The Winthrop Fleet of 1630

MAP SHOWING NUMBER OF PASSENGERS FROM EACH ENGLISH
COUNTY IN THE WINTHROP FLEET

Note: London and vicinity furnished 146 passengers

THE WINTHROP FLEET
of 1630

An *Account* of the VESSELS, the VOYAGE, the
PASSENGERS and their *English Homes*
from *Original Authorities*

By
CHARLES EDWARD BANKS

Member of the MASSACHUSETTS HISTORICAL SOCIETY
and of the AMERICAN ANTIQUARIAN SOCIETY

Originally published: 1930
Reprinted: Genealogical Publishing Co., Inc.
1001 N. Calvert St., Baltimore, Md. 21202
1961, 1968, 1972, 1976, 1980, 1983, 1989, 1994, 1999, 2003
Library of Congress Catalogue Card Number 68-57851
International Standard Book Number 0-8063-0020-5
Made in the United States of America

CONTENTS

PREFACE

IT is not a rhetorical exaggeration in idea to say that the militant Norman hosts who invaded England in 1066 with the Conqueror and the unarmed flotilla which brought the seven hundred Britons to New England in 1630 should be placed in the same historical framing as men who began distinct epochs in mediæval and modern times. Their objects, it is true, were different. One went to subdue the inhabitants in a military invasion, and the other to found a colony by peaceful penetration, bearing an olive branch of good will to the ancient occupants of the soil. The story of the Norman Conquest belongs to the period of picturesque chivalry and the names of the companions of William, Duke of Normandy, are enrolled on illuminated parchments among the historic treasures of Battle Abbey. All the great official documents of that realm for four centuries were dated as 'after the Conquest,' and the names of those who participated in this invasion are now held in perpetual remembrance.

The story of the passengers of the Winthrop Fleet requires no romantic narration nor suggests any of the qualities of military glory. Aside from a few professional soldiers hired to lead them when necessities of defense required it, these yeomen in fustian jackets and pot hats, and a few of the gentry in braver raiment, present an uninteresting and drab picture in comparison to the invading Norman knights weighted with casque, breastplate, and cuisse. Beyond the names of the few leaders no complete record of those who sailed in the Fleet led by Winthrop in the flagship *Arbella* is known to exist. It is highly improbable that such a one

was

was ever made similar to that recorded by Bradford of the *Mayflower* passengers of 1620, in his 'History of Plymouth Plantation.' He saved from oblivion the names of those simple Pilgrims who never dreamed of the historic immortality which his thoughtfulness has secured to them. To Winthrop can be given the credit, however, for placing on record the story of the voyage in diary form.

The object of this book is to rescue from future loss the names of all those who can be, with reasonable proof, certified as companions of the peaceful leader who brought them across the Atlantic to help found a new nation. They took part in the conquest of a continent — not in the enslavement of its inhabitants. This compilation has been completed after an extensive, as well as intensive, study of all classes of records, printed and in manuscript, bearing on this subject in the Colonial, County, and Town Records of Massachusetts. Supplementing this the author spent four years in England in researches relating to the ancestry and homes of these emigrants, and this feature of the work, never before undertaken on so large a scale, gives it a distinctive character. It has not been possible to supply the ancestry and origin of all of the passengers, for many of them were of humble and obscure social station whose names rarely ever reached the public records. It is to be said that the English homes and ancestors of a number of these persons are already known and this information has been incorporated, with reference to authorities in each case, to make the record complete. The investigations of the author are special additions which help make the topographical picture of the origin of this company more comprehensive and the maps which illustrate this feature should greatly aid in a graphic understanding of the local sources of the 'Great Emigration.'

Fortunately,

Fortunately, the wide knowledge of Mr. Charles Knowles Bolton could be made available in his studies of the earlier emigrants to New England who preceded the Winthrop Fleet, recently published, as well as personally communicated in frequent consultations. His advice on the general phases of the subject of English emigration in Colonial times has been supplemented by that of Mr. Clarence Almon Torrey on the many individual problems arising during the final stages of the work. Mr. Worthington Chauncey Ford, to whom the project was first broached, encouraged the undertaking, and when completed it received his approval and benediction, and the author hopes it will confirm his judgment that it is a worth-while contribution to the history of the beginnings of New England.

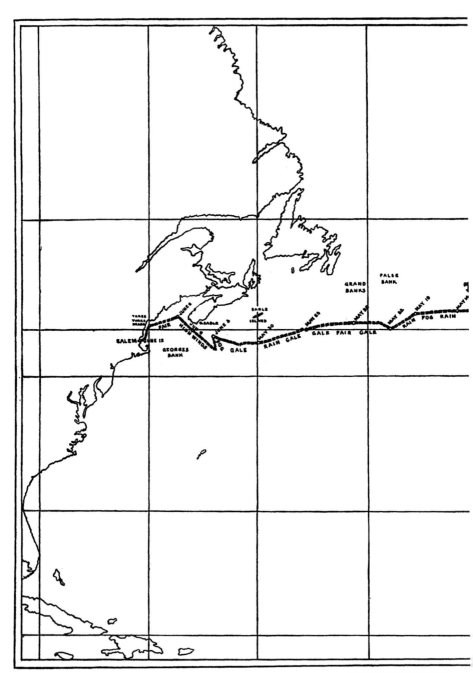

CHART OF THE COURSE

HEAVY WEATHER
43°18' N. LATITUDE
GALE
MAY 8
GALE
MAY 5
APR 29
APR 30
CALM
APR 28
APR 27
CALM
APR 26
APR 25
CALM
APR 24
APR 23
RAIN FOG STORMY FAIR
APR 18
APR 17
SCILLY IS.
GALE FAIR
CALM
APR 16
APR 11

CORVOS
AZORES
TERCEIRA

OF THE ARBELLA

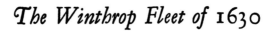

The Winthrop Fleet of 1630

THE WINTHROP FLEET
of 1630

• •

CHAPTER I

Setting the Stage

SINCE the early dawn of the century which saw the end of the reign of Elizabeth, England's greatest monarch, and the accession to her throne of James, 'the wisest fool in Christendom,' the mighty possibilities of imperial expansion set in motion by the explorations of Frobisher, Raleigh, Drake, Gilbert, Gosnold, and Weymouth had been coming to the next logical step in their natural development. After discovery occupation must follow. Within the first decade of the seventeenth century these adventurous men of our race were crossing the thousand leagues of the 'vast and furious ocean' which separated Europe from the almost unknown continent of North America. Beginning the year before the senile queen 'of famous memory' was on her death-couch, the earliest colony set out from Falmouth, County Cornwall, to make a trial of settlement on the shores of New England. Each succeeding year marked the departure of a like expedition to get a foothold on our dangerous and forbidding littoral. Failure followed failure of these persistent voyagers to accomplish their designs of permanency. The rigorous winter climate to which they were not enured helped to cool their enthusiasm to conquer it after enjoying the novel delights of our spring, summer, and autumn temperatures. Gosnold, who

first

first essayed in 1602 to challenge the sovereignty of this region for the abode of the white man, retired in good order after a few months at Cuttyhunk on the Elizabeth Islands.[1] Pring in 1603 established a short acquaintance with the harbor which was to become the permanent home of an experimental socialist plantation seventeen years later, but he, too, gracefully retired when the early frosts reminded him of that season when a white Christmas was the inevitable programme of the forces of Nature with which they could not comfortably cope.[2] In 1605, Weymouth added to their needed knowledge of the topography of the Maine coast, planted crosses here and there in token of seizure in the name of his sovereign, and laid the foundation for the first serious attempt to occupy the claims he had staked out. He also joined the list of temporary sojourners on our rocky coast-line.[3]

The year 1607 witnessed two determined attempts to solve this growing problem of acquiring a permanent foothold for Englishmen on this continent. Already the French had solved it in Canada and the Spanish in Florida, and it came to be a race for empire from 34° to 45°, North Latitude, or fight. Two chartered companies set out in the spring of this year — one under the patronage of the Plymouth or Northern Company for the better-known and more explored territory of the Maine coast. Three vessels, the *Sarah Constant*, the *Discovery*, and the *Goodspeed* took colonists to the James River in Virginia and began the Southern Colony at Jamestown. The pleasant climate of that region contributed to the success of this planting and it became the first permanent settlement of Englishmen in our present national limits

[1] Purchas: *Pilgrimes* (ed. Glasgow, 1905), xviii, 302.
[2] *Ibid.*, 322–28.
[3] Burrage: *Weymouth's Voyage* (Gorges Society), *passim*.

limits.[1] Simultaneously from Plymouth, under the patronage of the Lord Chief Justice of England and Sir Ferdinando Gorges, the Gilberts and other West-Country men, two vessels — the *Mary and John* and the *Gift of God* — turned their prows hopefully to the 'stern and rock-bound coast' of Maine where the Kennebec empties its waters into the broad Atlantic. Theirs was the more difficult task and was undertaken by men almost unfitted for the serious task. The leader, Captain George Popham, of Bridgewater, of three-score years and ten, was chosen to promote an enterprise that called for the vigor of youth. He died during the first winter and his bones remain unlocated on the bleak and rocky promontory of Sabino, overlooking the restless ocean which he had but recently crossed. No more uninviting spot could have been chosen for the site of a colony. Yet it survived an exceptionally severe winter with no other casualty, and a fort was constructed for permanent protection. The little colony continued to function during the following spring and summer, but the ships sent to England for supplies brought back news of the death of Chief Justice Popham, its chief supporter, and of another patron, brother of Raleigh Gilbert, Esq., of Marldon, Devon, who had been chosen Vice-Governor of the Colony, and these events with other contributing causes resulted in the abandonment of this first well-organized plan to conquer the relentless winter climate of New England among its barren spaces. This failure was attributed to these natural obstacles to successful planting of a colony in that region and practically ended for the next decade all concerted attempts to win that inhospitable region to serve the uses of the white man.[2] The 'sea-dogs'

[1] Smith: *History of Virginia.*

[2] Thayer: *Voyage to Sagadahoc* (Gorges Society), 87–156. Further reference may be made to the author's presentation of new documents on this colony to the *Antiquarian Society*, xxxix, part 2.

dogs' of Devon had solved the initial factors in the problem of bringing this continent to the knowledge of their nation, but had not been able to utilize its vast potentialities for the service of mankind. The reputation of that region as a home for Englishmen was blasted by the failure of the Popham Colony to maintain occupation beyond a twelvemonth, albeit the abandonment was in reality due to internal and personal causes and not to insurmountable external elements. Nevertheless, one great source of attraction became the magnet which continued to draw these dauntless mariners to our coast yearly in increasing numbers. They came in by the score to lure wealth from the virgin fishing-grounds, where codfish were so plentiful that, as one expressed it, they 'pestered' the vessels in shoals. Soon there grew up fishing stations and permanent establishments at Monhegan, Pemaquid, and Damariscove, where the curing of fish became a valuable industry. Vessels from the Southern Colony at Jamestown came hither to obtain sea-food for their winter subsistence and the coast of Maine was a busy place in the height of the fishing season. To abandon such a source of wealth to the savages or to their European rivals was a concession to weakness which was not a fundamental quality in the spirits of men who could ride the waves for weeks to reach this new land. Again in 1616 one of the great figures in the colonization movements of the past, Sir Ferdinando Gorges, determined to verify his belief that this winter climate of Northern Virginia, as it was then called, was inhabitable by Englishmen. He sent a party to spend the winter months at the mouth of the Saco River, and when they came back in the spring to tell their experiences, the old accepted legend was permanently shattered. Henceforth it was judged to be suitable for occupancy the year round and the great fishing fleets confirmed it by establishing

permanent

permanent quarters for their industries on the Maine coast.[1]
Meanwhile developments went on apace in natural se-
quence. The little band of religious zealots who had left
their native land in 1610 for religious freedom in Holland
began to think of their future under an alien flag, and fell to
considering a second migration to the unsettled continent
beyond the Western ocean where they could once more live
under their own flag and bring up their children in the language of their fathers. Over there they could have land in
plenty, start life anew as Englishmen, and found a religious
colony modeled on their own design. In 1620 they came in
the immortal ship, the *Mayflower*, from Leyden, reënforced
by threescore and more of London folk to join them in establishing a socialist plantation, financed by Merchant Adventurers of the great city. The story of these first 'Pilgrims'
is too well known to be retold here; but the unsanitary conditions of travel at sea, the lack of proper food causing
scurvy, and the rigors of winter brought a toll of fifty victims
the first winter — half the little company unsheltered in
their poorly constructed shacks or huddled in the stuffy
cabins of the ship. Yet they were forced to remain to conquer or die. They had burned their bridges behind them in
Holland and could not return to England, where they would
be questioned for religious contumacy. Reënforced the next
year by additions of nearly twoscore Londoners from a second
ship, the *Fortune*, and in 1623 by a third ship, the *Anne*, the
loss in numbers was more than made up, and for the next
seven years they prospered and slowly grew to be the largest
body of Englishmen in one settlement on the coast of Massachusetts.[2] Small and casual parties of the courageous breed
of

[1] Gorges: *Briefe Narration*, 57–62.

[2] Bradford: *History of Plimmoth Plantation, passim.* The results of researches for
the origins of the passengers of these three ships, similar to that undertaken for the
Winthrop Fleet, may be found in the author's *English Ancestry and Homes of the
Pilgrim Fathers.* (Grafton Press, New York, 1929.)

of Englishmen followed them hither to lay claim to the soil for themselves and for the glory of the Kingdom. Settlements were made in Weymouth (1623), at Braintree (1623), at Winnisimmet, Nantasket, and in Boston Harbor (1624), at Naumkeag (1624), Shawmut (1624), and Mishawum (1625) — little clearings in the great forest that fringed the coast-line from Cape Cod to Cape Ann. Contemporaneously the mouth of the Piscataqua gave hospitality to like squatters in that region and so formed a connecting link with the busier settlements now growing larger and more important on the Maine coast. At Damariscove Island a fully equipped settlement of fishermen, protected by a palisade of logs ten feet high, bade defiance to Indian arrows and French muskets. Monhegan was the farthest outpost to the eastward.[1] These were all individual groups independent of each other, and in splendid isolation the band of religious sectaries from Leyden held themselves apart from all of them, for these other settlers were 'worldly people' brought up in the rites of the Established Church and having no sympathy with or part in the programme of the Plymouth Separatists. Perhaps the total of all these groups would number five hundred souls, subjects of the King, but bound together by no other ties. They cut little or no figure in the national consciousness and were scarcely mentioned in the talk of the times beyond the counting-houses of the merchants who were financially interested in the several ventures at these scattered points. Patents of territory had been taken to cover some of these enterprises, but they added nothing to the importance of the squatter sovereignty to which they belonged. Some of these patents were never confirmed or completed by actual settlement and others of them had limits impossible to
define

[1] The latest and best authority on these early and scattered seacoast settlements is Bolton's *Real Founders of New England* (Boston, 1929).

define or were overlapped by grants that had little reference to prior occupancy.

Thus, by gradual and persistent effort to overcome baffling obstacles hitherto unknown to Englishmen, the coast of Massachusetts came gradually into the actual possession of white men in the space of twenty-seven years after Gosnold had made his summer residence on Cuttyhunk. All these successive footholds gained by venturous Britons made the background and setting for the larger and more important act in the drama of American colonization — the Great Migration of 1630, from another part of England which hitherto had not shared in the preliminary scenes here related.

CHAPTER II

The Background

WHAT had been going on in the material life of
England since the accession of James, in the ex-
tension and expansion of its commercial interests
overseas and the consciousness of the imperial destiny in
seeking for new outlets for the national growth, was having
its parallel in the spiritual development of the age. The
effects of the Reformation, first finding definite expression
less than a century before, were being formulated slowly,
characteristic of the English mentality. Reforming the religious habits of generations was a halting and painful process
for our ancestors, and the Church 'by law established,'
having inherited the status of the old Papal organization
with its compact body of ecclesiastics, was always prepared
to battle for their prerogatives under any system of theology.
This period, well up to 1600, was occupied by the protesting
element to slough off all the remnants of Romish rites, while
Catholic Mary and Protestant Elizabeth were engaged in
killing off each other's heretics. But the domination of
foreign friars and alien abbots had practically ceased when
the new century opened. The release from their sordid grip
gave opportunities, untrammeled, for that religious freedom
which the people were too ignorant and unprepared to use
with discretion. It became a fresh and unlimited field for the
exploitation of self-educated theologians unrestrained by the
authorities. The Bible placed in the hands of the common
people became the fount and source of myriads of whimsical
doctrines fashioned out of 'Holy Writ' and interpreted by
these amateur expositors. These reformers undertook not
only

only to transform and destroy the symbolism of the Church, but to reconstruct the fundamental doctrines of Christian theology. The liturgy of the Mass was revamped by excising every Romish rite and often transforming it into a meaningless gesture. The sacrament of baptism furnished the most fertile field for the ingenuity of unlettered Biblical microscopists, and Pedobaptists, Anabaptists, and Se-Baptists emerged from this welter of verbal tergiversations on that fundamental of Christianity alone. Of course, the Holy Communion was stripped of its attributes in adoration of the real Presence as taught by the Romish Church and with them went most of the respectful conduct of the protesting sects toward this rite during its solemnization. These antagonists not only refused to partake of the Lord's Supper, but to show their hostility refused to take off their hats while it was being administered. Absence from the church services naturally followed, and during the first quarter of this century the Archdeacons' Courts were busy dealing with acts of contumacy ranging from non-attendance at worship to acts of disrespect during services. The Bishops' Courts were equally busy in dealing with the acts of the delinquent clergy. The situation favored the loosening of all beliefs in doctrines and ceremonies. The laity were not 'persecuted,' as is the common legend. They were dealt with by the local ecclesiastics and merely given reprimands, orders to make public confession of their fault, or excommunication if recalcitrant. The clergy were subjected to more serious hazards, as in disobeying the church laws they were violating their oaths given at ordination, and it is to be remembered that Church and State being one they were breaking the laws of the realm. These refractory ministers who refused to follow the canon law and disobeyed the orders of the Bishop with respect to the sacraments were fined and sometimes imprisoned if they
proved

proved recalcitrant. Being deprived of their appointments, their means of living was taken away. While many of the clergy were sincere in their opposition to the constituted authorities, the disturbances of the times gave opportunities for clerical demagogues to play up to the prejudices of the mob and stage spectacular scenes in churches. In one place the town authorities employed one of these mountebanks as preacher to harangue the people in the afternoons. He would use the sermon delivered in the morning by the Vicar as a text for his lampoons and make sport of it in coarse and ribald language. He was tried before the Bishop, found guilty of disorderly conduct, and then fled to New England as a 'persecuted' clergyman to escape his fines.·

In no section of England was the spirit of hostility to the Established Church more widely spread and more deeply ingrained than in the section known as East Anglia, comprising the counties of Norfolk, Suffolk, and Essex. Of course there were no exact comital lines which embraced these Puritan sectaries, as the adjoining counties of Cambridge, Herts, Middlesex, and London itself were inoculated with the same 'heresies.' Cambridge University was the Alma Mater of most of the dissenting clergy and certainly of the vast majority of those ministers who emigrated to New England. They were the 'scofflaws' of their generation and became the irreconcilable intolerants in the religious discussions of the first quarter of that century. East Anglia became the early nursery of the dissenters and the consistent supporter of the clandestine congregations which grew up in that region. They were called by several names — Brownists, Independents, Separatists; but by whatever title known, although differing in methods and dogmas, they were unanimous in opposition to the Established Church and generally at loggerheads with each other. Out of this region

region were enlisted the first volunteers of that great army of emigrants who shook the dust of England from their feet in the twenty years preceding the death of King Charles (1649).

It is not, however, a correct assumption to picture these emigrants as leaving their ancestral homes because of the religious unrest of the times. Only a portion of them were motivated by this reason and it is doubtful if it were the real preponderating influence in this great movement. There were other more substantial factors operating, economic and social. The majority of these people were of the yeoman class who for generations had been the tenantry of the nobility and landed gentry. They did not live — they simply vegetated, hopeless of any improvement in their condition socially or materially, and doomed to support indefinitely a class of parasites set over them by a monarchical form of government. The Manorial System perpetuated a social slavery whereby landlords drained the earnings of their tenants, whose lives were spent in working for their masters and who died as poor as they began. The servile section of the clergy preached to these patient plodders the doctrine of Christian resignation and acceptance of the lot in which Providence had placed them. It was a contemptible part of the 'system' which helped to condemn the so-called 'lower classes' to hopeless serfdom with the sanction of the Church and the approval of Holy Writ. Only in rare instances could a tenant become a freeholder, and, coincident with the acquirement of his spiritual freedom, these downtrodden yeomen came to sense their opportunity for material liberty, their right to profit by the toil of their hands. This right was being gradually recognized as inevitable during the reign of James the First, and when Charles the First came to the throne, his extreme views of the Royal Prerogative began to
wreck

wreck their newly acquired privileges. The extravagances of Charles's Court and his imposition of taxes without the authority of Parliament to meet these excessive charges led to resistance from all classes. Large and small freeholders were the victims of taxation illegally laid on their holdings. In this class were the recently emancipated tenants, who found themselves taxed unjustly by a King who flouted their Parliament and set up an arbitrary government. It presaged civil war.

Among the other restless spirits were those whose land hunger was not satisfied. They could not become free men in the fullest meaning. They knew of the great continent across the Atlantic where a hundred acres would be given to each and every settler — a king's ransom in their vocabulary and almost beyond their conception as a reality. There they would, indeed, be free to enter into a new existence unhampered by the dead hand of precedents and the remorseless exactions of the landed gentry. Although technically the plantations in this new country would be under the jurisdiction of the English authorities, yet they would inevitably become disentangled from all the traditions of the past, and the opportunity to establish a liberal commonwealth was the great aspiration of those who had the courage to break away from the land of their fathers, cross an uncharted ocean, and encounter unknown perils from a savage race and from the wild beasts of the trackless forests. This is the background out of which the Great Emigration emerged.[1]

[1] The specific authorities for the variety of statements made in this description of the social and religious conditions in England are too numerous for citation. They have been derived from many contemporaneous books and modern interpretations of them, but particular acknowledgment is due to Dexter's *England and Holland of the Pilgrims,* 3–188, which deals with this whole historical development. The author was affiliated with the Congregational Church, but presented his views without bias.

CHAPTER III

Preparing for the Hegira

THE ways and means by which these various eager and restless spirits were organized for this great adventure and became the *dramatis personae* of transcendental importance deserve particular study. It must be borne in mind that, while they became pioneers of a distinct exodus of people from their ancestral homes, they were not the first who had essayed this trying ordeal on the American coast. English colonists had made homes for themselves in Virginia since 1607 and prospered, and for ten years the little band of Pilgrims at Plymouth had struggled and won a foothold on the drear and infertile coast in what is now known as the Old Colony. The accomplishments of these hardy tenants of an inhospitable region, scarcely numbering more than a few hundred, had made no distinctive impression upon the knowledge of Englishmen. The Plymouth Plantation was almost unknown and scarcely ever mentioned in the daily life and conversation of the common people of England. In a sense, therefore, those to whom was presented the project of joining an emigration movement across the Atlantic considered it a novel idea. But little printed material was available on the subject. The few 'narratives' on the Virginia and Plymouth settlements rarely found readers in the small parishes of the English countryside. What little these yeomen knew of the country which came to be called 'New England' filtered down to them through the medium of the local clergy, especially those who were becoming detached from their loyalty to the established religion. These vicars and curates who were beginning

ginning to feel the restraining hand of the hierarchy on their growing habits of nonconformity to the rites and doctrines of the Established Church were indirectly the instigators of this migratory movement. It was these ecclesiastical recusants who had brought down on themselves the disciplinary machinery of the Church for their contumacy, and finding their functions suspended, their incomes cut off, and their civil status imperiled, encouraged the hope of greater opportunities in a new land to carry on their independent ministrations beyond the reach of the King's and Lord's officials. Yet with this generalization we do not answer the natural inquiry as to the methods by which individuals in widely separated parts of England were gathered in one group under acknowledged leaders to take part in this self-imposed exile from their homes and native land. The historic index points unerringly to the Reverend John White, of Dorsetshire, England, as the earliest and most important original factor among the influences which led up to this new colonizing company. Generally known as the 'Patriarch of Dorchester' [England], he had been continuously at the head of various organized companies as well as unorganized movements to effect settlements on the Massachusetts coast. This work he began in 1623 with the Dorchester Company, which took possession of Cape Ann as a site for a colony, and thereafter he was identified with every like development on the coast, and was interested in every company that finally became merged successively into this last great venture in 1629 — the Massachusetts Bay Company. White was a conforming Puritan of liberal views. He recognized the need of dealing with the large hostile sentiment then existing against the Established Church and believed that the emigration of these Dissenters to a new country not only would afford a remedy for their grievances, but answer the growing pres-

sure

sure of adverse economic conditions. He further believed it would be an indirect advantage to England itself in relieving it of the agitations of a dissatisfied element, restoring peace at home and at the same time giving the emigrants a safety valve for their opposition to expend itself. His whole thought was to employ this means to heal a growing discontent, spiritual and material, which was plaguing the English people. In later years he is found condemning the excesses of these people in Massachusetts in their persecution of others in the name of religion.[1]

In support of his early plans for the settlement of the coast of Massachusetts Bay, he had enlisted scores of prominent men in the West Country — Dorset, Somerset, and Devon — as stockholders. Among them was Colonel John Humphrey, son of Michael Humphrey, gentleman, of Chaldon, County Dorset. Colonel Humphrey was a familiar figure in London and connected by marriage with Lord de la Warr and the Pelham family, both associated with colonization projects. For his third wife Humphrey married in 1630 the Lady Susan Fiennes, daughter of the Earl of Lincoln, sister of the Lady Arbella, wife of Isaac Johnson, and of like kinship to John Gorges, the son of Sir Ferdinando. Thus a definite contact can be established between the earliest colonizing projects started by White and this last one, the goal of his efforts. It is possible to visualize the association of Humphrey with the Earl of Lincoln's family connection which played such an important part in the development of this climax of White's work. Through it we can account for Thomas Dudley, a retainer of the Earl, but a native of Northamptonshire, as a passenger in this fleet.

Sempringham

---

[1] The author has had the privilege of reading advance sheets of the *Life of Reverend John White*, by Frances Rose-Troup, from which this brief view of his pioneer labors in the founding of Massachusetts is taken.

Sempringham, in Lincolnshire, the seat of the Earl, had already the year before sent forth to Salem in New England its Rector, the Reverend Samuel Skelton, and thus, like a pebble thrown into a pool, the influence of John White of Dorchester reached out in widening ripples.

Just how Winthrop was drawn into the project is uncertain. He was a late recruit in the scheme. In fact, the Massachusetts Bay Company had been in existence a year and a half before the name of the elder Winthrop appears on the records. Prior to that, however, in April, 1628, John Winthrop, Jr., had under consideration the plan of going to New England on some sort of an expedition thither for business or investigation. In a letter to his father at that time he wrote: 'For my voyage to New England, I doe not resolve, (especially following my Uncle [Emanuel] Downing's advice), except I misse the Straightes (Gibraltar) but I will stay till you have sold the land though I misse of both.' Thus New England had been discussed in the family circles.

Three months later the younger Winthrop was at Leghorn on his voyage to Mediterranean ports, and that was the end of that earlier idea of going to New England. The seed, however, was working and in his frequent visits to London as one of the attorneys of the Court of Wards and Liveries,[1] the elder Winthrop would be brought into contact through his brother-in-law Downing, not only with some of the active members of the newly chartered Company of the Massachusetts Bay, particularly Isaac Johnson, but with other like projects in the Caribbean Islands undertaken by his kinsman and county neighbors. His son Henry had already gone to the Barbados to establish himself in that island colony. The times were beginning to be stirring politically. The

[1] He was admitted with Emanuel Downing, 29 June, 1628 (Records of the Inner Temple, II, 169).

The King had dissolved Parliament, which was not to meet again for more than a decade, and he was sorting out the lukewarm among his subjects as well as his open enemies for reprisals. Writing to his wife in May, 1629, the Squire of Groton Manor poured out his apprehensions as to the future of the country and his own fortunes. 'I am verilye persuaded God will bring some heavye Affliction upon this lande and that speedylie.'[1] The blow fell upon him the next month when he was deprived of his office of Attorney in the Court of Wards and Liveries, with its large and welcome fees and this, added to his financial burden, caused him to exclaim to his wife, 'Where we shall spend the rest of our short tyme I knowe not: the Lorde, I trust, will direct us in mercye.'[2] At this critical time, in his anxiety for his own future, an argument in manuscript, 'Reasons for and against settling a plantation in New England,' was circulated among the group of Puritans who were known to have supported the colonization projects begun by White. A copy came to the notice of Winthrop and at his request his son Forth made a copy for the Governor's use.[3]

By the summer of 1629, Winthrop had practically decided to throw in his lot with the Massachusetts Bay Company. His reasons as stated in his family letters were the constantly increasing expenses of a grown and growing family with no prospects of additional income and the urgency of the stockholders in the Company that he undertake the leadership of the organization. 'If he lett pass this opportunitie,' he recorded on a personal memorandum, 'that talent which God

---

[1] *L. & L. W.*, 1, 296.   [2] *Ibid.*, 1, 214, 301.

[3] It is believed on good internal evidence that it was prepared by White himself, as from the circumstances Winthrop could hardly have been its author, as claimed by his distinguished descendant, the late Robert Charles Winthrop in his *Life and Letters of John Winthrop*, 1, 308, 328. A contemporary copy is in the Winthrop MSS. in the Library of the Massachusetts Historical Society.

God hath bestowed uppon him for publicke service is like to be buried.'[1] Whether this pessimistic view of his chances of development and success at home was justified is an unanswerable question, but it is clear that his decision was based on material rather than spiritual grounds. He said nothing that indicates his dissatisfaction with the Established Church. In none of his later writings has he left any suggestion that ecclesiastical persecution or distasteful teachings or ritualistic practices influenced his decision to sell the family manor and the comforts of its appointments to start life anew in an unknown wilderness on an almost unknown continent. By his own testimony it was a question of pounds, shillings, and pence, of a decreasing income and an unfavorable balance-sheet, which led him to flee from a political and economic situation which others remained to fight and win in the end. It is pure speculation to surmise what he might have become in the next decade as the Puritan power became dominant. A lawyer of his talents and character might have been among the chief advisers of Cromwell and after the death of Charles one of the great officers of State.

In July, 1629, a few weeks after he had lost his office, Winthrop and his brother-in-law, Emanuel Downing, attended a meeting at Sempringham by invitation of Isaac Johnson, the husband of the Lady Arbella, to discuss the subject of emigration to America, either New England or the West India Islands. The decision favored the former place, and on August 26, at a second conference in the University town of Cambridge, Sir Richard Saltonstall, Thomas Dudley, William Vassall, Nicholas West, Increase Nowell, Isaac Johnson, John Humphrey, Thomas Sharpe, John Winthrop, William Colborne, Kellam Browne, and William Pynchon concluded an agreement to go to New England by the

[1] 1 *Mass. Hist. Soc. Proc.*, VIII, 420; comp. *Life and Letters of Winthrop*, I, 327.

the first of the following March (1629–30), with their families and personal property, and establish a plantation there for permanent settlement. Thus John Winthrop, Lord of the Manor of Groton, came at last to the turning-point of his career and, casting his lot with these men, soon attained leadership. His name has become attached to the fleet which was the first fruits of the great project that resulted in the Puritan settlement of New England.

Winthrop's first attendance was at a meeting of the Company on October 15, 1629, and five days later he was chosen Governor 'for his integritie & sufficiencie.' Humphrey was elected Deputy Governor at the same meeting, at which the Reverend John White was present, showing his continued interest in the plans and his support of them. From this date forward the ensuing six months were busy times for the promoters. They were employed in spreading far and wide the gospel of emigration and signing up recruits for the passenger list. Naturally, the 'underground telegraph' of what was in prospect reached all sorts of persons ready for the adventure, for one reason or another, but it found responses more readily among those sympathetically inclined to Puritan and Separatist ideas. The Dissenting and Separatist clergy were already in touch with each other and were early informed of the nature and purposes of the project, and those who were out of a job or earning a precarious living by school teaching or holding services surreptitiously in private houses were thought to be fit subjects for the new propaganda, but they did not join this first great hegira. Archbishop Laud, their Nemesis later, had not come into power when this movement was being organized, and not for several years later were the clergy harried by his Grace and his High Commission Court. Only two regular clergymen came with Winthrop — the Reverend John Wilson, a native
of

of Windsor, Berkshire, who had been preaching at Sudbury, Suffolk, and the Reverend George Phillips, similarly employed at Boxford in the same county, within six miles of each other with Groton between the two.[1] Their inclusion in this company may be credited to the personal influence of Winthrop, and Phillips was a fellow passenger in the *Arbella*. The Michaelmas and Hilary Assizes of 1629 at Bury St. Edmunds, always largely attended by the yeomanry of the county, gave Winthrop an opportunity to meet many persons who would be informed of the proposed plantation in New England, and thus the gospel of a new country where land could be had freely and held in fee simple was placed before the tenantry of Suffolk under favorable circumstances and with good results. While it was generally understood that the leaders of this movement were sympathizers with the reform element in the Established Church, yet this feature was not presented as an inducement, and from what is known of subsequent happenings, it is clear that a considerable part of the passengers of the Winthrop Fleet were loyal to the English Church and had no intent or desire to be a part of any scheme that pretended otherwise. A contemporary writer alleged that 'divers went under the Umbrella of Religion.'[2] Many of them never joined the Puritan churches, nor became Freemen after their arrival.

That the whole task of advertising the programme of the Company did not devolve on Winthrop is in evidence, but we have knowledge of his writing personal letters to 'prospects' in various parts of England. In London, where the work

---

[1] Giles Saxton, who was on a jury in September, 1630, and made Freeman in 1631, is presumed to be identical with the Reverend Giles Saxton, a Yorkshireman, studious and learned, who resided at Scituate and Boston. He later returned to Leeds, England. (*L.P.D.*, comp. Cotton Mather.) This would make three clergymen who came with the Fleet.

[2] Gardiner: *New England's Vindication* (1660), 3.

work of preparation was centered, the labor was done by a few at Governor Cradock's house on Cannon Street near London Stone. Deputy Governor Goffe's house on East Cheap, Isaac Johnson's residence in Soper Lane, Mr. Increase Nowell's house in Philpot Lane near by, and doubtless Emanual Downing's house in Peterborough Court, off Fleet Street (where Winthrop made his home in the City), were the centers of much missionary work among persons inquiring about the new colony overseas. It is doubtful if printed appeals were circulated by the promoters, yet a diarist of the period stated that 'Books of Incouragement' were distributed in various parts of England; but if so none have survived, and the writer may refer to tracts that were printed after their departure.[1] Nevertheless, the work of the promoters was well done by word of mouth, and toward the end of the campaign they were able to exercise their privilege of rejecting some applicants and of making choice of certain artisans who would be necessary in establishing a new colony.

[1] John Rous noted in his Diary, under date of June 7, 1630: 'I sawe a book at Bury [St. Edmund] at a book-sellers, conteining a declaration of their intent who be gone to Newe England, set out by themselves, and prepared for satisfaction to the King and State (as I conceive) because of some scandalous misconceivings that runne abroade.' (Camden Society, LVI, 54.)

CHAPTER IV

Expense of Travel and Supplies

PASSENGER travel across the North Atlantic Ocean, which is now one of the great enterprises of maritime business, may with truth be said to have started with the departure of the Winthrop Fleet. It carried, as has been stated, the largest number of Englishmen sailing as passengers in one body across the Atlantic up to that event. There had been no occasion for such a large group of emigrants to require the services of a fleet of vessels. Since that event there has been constant movement of vessels carrying passengers between the European and American shores. The maritime interests of England were entirely concerned with exports and imports and passenger travel was merely incidental to this extensive overseas trade. Ships were not built to accommodate travelers and those who desired to visit foreign countries had to adjust themselves to the inconveniences of a freight-carrying vessel. Nor had this new traffic as yet resulted in any modification of the interior construction of vessels to make them more comfortable for their human freight. The eleven vessels secured for carrying the Great Emigration were the ordinary freighters of the period. There were certain vessels engaged in the wine trade to the Mediterranean ports which, by reason of their occupation, were specially constructed and were known as 'sweet ships,' as they were unusually well caulked and always dry. The *Mayflower* was of this type and it is probable that the vessels of the Winthrop Fleet on which passengers were mainly carried were selected from this class of traders. A certain number of them carried only horses, cattle, and small stock.

The

The construction and model of these ships are shown in the accompanying illustrations of a typical craft of the early seventeenth century. The bow with the high forecastle deck was occupied by the seamen before the mast, and the still higher poop deck on the stern which covered the cabin sheltered the quarters of the officers. The space between these two towering structures, or 'between decks,' which was open on small vessels or fitted with a deck and a hold in large craft, was used for the cargo, the ordnance and stowing of the long boats. In this part of the ship, as we learn from Winthrop's story, 'some cabins' had been constructed, probably rough compartments of boards for women and children, while hammocks for the men were swung from every available point of vantage. We may be assured that Lady Arbella Johnson and some of 'the better quality' had special quarters in the cabins, as we are told that they were changed to the lower deck for safety during the threatened hostilities, meaning the 'hold' or 'between decks.' It may be left to the imagination how the sanitary needs of the passengers were met in ordinary weather with smooth seas. It would be merely speculation to know how the requirements of nature were met in prolonged storms for the women and children were kept under the hatches.

The number of passengers in the Winthrop Fleet will be discussed elsewhere, but in addition to the number of 'souls' comprising the emigrants were the officers and crews of the several ships. It is recorded that the *Arbella* (350 tons) was 'manned with fifty-two seamen,' but the number of officers is not given, probably not less than fifteen of all ranks. This is the only basis we have for estimating the number of persons engaged in navigating the eleven ships and it must be necessarily proximate. From all the circumstances of the problem it may be assumed that the *Arbella* was the largest ship

ship and with that allowance not less than four hundred officers and seamen manned the entire fleet and, thus figured, there were not less than eleven hundred stowed away in these ships, perhaps an average of a hundred to each one. The cost of transportation overseas for passengers was somewhat of a new problem in maritime reckoning, as the length of the voyage was always uncertain, sometimes ranging in length from six to twelve weeks. The people emigrating in this Fleet were to be carried under an arrangement with the Company 'at the rate of 5 li. a person.'[1] William Wood, a contemporary writer, said on this point: 'Every man have ship-provisions allowed him for his five pounds a man, which is Salt Beefe, Porke, Salt Fish, Butter, Cheese, Pease Pottage, Water-grewell, and such kind of Victuals, with good Biskets, and sixe-shilling Beere.' This, of course, was for adults, and for children the following schedule of relative fares was provided:

> Sucking children not to bee reckoned; such as under 4 yeares of age, 3 for one [fare]; under 8, 2 for one; under 12, 3 for 2.[2]

It is understood that each emigrant traveled at his own expense for himself and those dependent upon him, and it should be here explained in this connection that there were four classes of emigrants: (1) those who paid for their passage over; (2) those who had some profession, art or trade and were to receive remuneration for same in money or grants of land; (3) those who paid a part of their passage and were to labor at the rate of three shillings a day after arrival in repayment; (4) indentured servants were carried at the expense of their masters, who were to receive in return fifty acres of land for each servant transported.[3] This was similar
to

---

[1] *Mass. Col. Recs.*, 1, 65. New England's Prospect, 42.   [2] *Ibid.*, 1, 66.
[3] *Ibid.*, 1, 29, 30, 34, 35, 77.

to the plan adopted in Virginia to encourage the bringing over of settlers. The cost of transportation was an important item in the consideration of the average tenant farmer or artisan, as the single fare reckoned at present values would be six or eight times as much, relatively, and was almost prohibitive for a large family.

In addition to the fares for passage the cost of shipping household goods increased the financial problem for the emigrant. It was necessary to carry these things as there was no way of obtaining them in an unsettled country. The rate for this service was fixed at '4 li a tonn for goods.' [1] For the average Puritan family of eight persons, with a ton of freight, the cost of the trip would be about thirty pounds, or nearly a thousand dollars in our present money.

In what manner the Lares and Penates of the passengers reached their destination may be surmised from the unfamiliarity of these husbandmen and artisans from East Anglia and London with the perils of the deep. Very few of them had ever left the shores of the 'tight little isle' and they were ignorant of the inadequacy of these absurdly small craft in the trough of the mountainous Atlantic seas developed in her savage moods. A contemporary writer speaks of the giant waves 'hurling their unfixed goods from place to place,' from lack of proper stowage.[2]

The present descendants of our first settlers have scant conception and practically no actual knowledge of the conditions which their ancestors experienced in making the long trans-Atlantic voyage from England to the American continent. The most that is understood and appreciated is the diminutive size of the vessels and the long and hazardous
passage

[1] *Mass. Col. Recs.*, I, 65. Higginson states that it cost £10 to ship a horse to New England.

[2] Johnson: *Wonder-Working Providence.*

passage required under the best conditions to reach the 'stern and rock-bound coast' of New England. The character and size of the vessels which composed this fleet have been described previously. Beyond that nothing definite is known as to their living accommodations, their food supplies and their existence under the uncomfortable conditions in cramped quarters.

In addition to the medical men emigrating as passengers — Doctors Gager and Palsgrave — there were undoubtedly physicians on each of the ships, which carried a considerable number of passengers, in accordance with maritime law. This medical service was an extra charge amounting to 2s 6d for each person covering the voyage. The regulations of the Guild of Barber Surgeons of that date (Sec. 47) specified that the 'furniture' (instruments, medicines, etc.) of surgeons employed at sea should be examined before sailing. The duties and qualifications of this official are thus defined by Captain John Smith in his *Accidence for Young Seamen* (London, 1626, p. 3):

> The *Chirurgeon* is exempted from all duty but to attend the sicke and cure the wounded; and good care would be had that he have a Certificate from the *Barber-Surgeons* Hall for his sufficiency, and also that his Chest bee well furnished both for *Physicke* and *Chirurgery* and so neare as may be proper for the clime you goe for, which neglect hath beene a losse of many a mans life.

In the then existing state of medical knowledge there was little scientific information regarding one of the great dangers of ocean voyages — the certainty of scurvy appearing if the voyage extended over six weeks without the opportunity of obtaining fresh vegetables. This morbid shadow hung over every project of overseas exploration and proved to be the undoing of many an expedition to unknown shores across the Atlantic.

Atlantic. It placed its deadly hand on the expeditions of Drake, Raleigh, and Gilbert, and only ten years before the Winthrop Fleet started, half of the *Mayflower* Pilgrims died of scorbutic starvation during the first few months after their arrival in Plymouth. There was little accurate knowledge of the cause of this dietary disease. It was vaguely understood that the lack of fresh vegetables was one of the factors in its causation, but they had no means of supplying this deficiency on prolonged voyages. It seems that Winthrop himself had been advised on this subject, for we find him writing back to his wife to bring 'a gallon of Scurvy grasse to drink a litle 5: or 6: morninges together, with some saltpeter dissolved in it & a litle grated or sliced nutmege.' [1] While limes and lemons were procurable their usefulness as prophylactics in scurvy was little known except among those who followed the sea. Their main reliance was on beer, which was therapeutically sound judgment, as it served both to allay thirst and as a mild anti-scorbutic. Water could not be preserved sweet and potable on these long voyages. For this reason we find that in the list of provisions for the *Arbella* forty-two tuns of beer were provided for the passengers of that ship (about ten thousand gallons).[2] There is nothing to indicate that limes or lemons were carried, as numbers fell victims to scurvy on the voyage and many after arrival died from the lack of proper preventives. This disease persisted for several months after landing, causing continuous mortality and it was not until the return of the *Lyon* in the

spring,

---

[1] 'Scurvy Grass,' a corruption of Scurvy Cress, is a cruciferous plant (*Cochlearia officinalis*) found in northern Europe in cultivation and in wild form in high latitudes in North America. Early used as an anti-scorbutic and later as a salad. 'Buy any scurvy-grass' may be read in *The Roaring Girl*, III, 2, by Middleton and Dekker.

[2] Memorandum on fly-leaves of Winthrop's Journal. Each vessel carried a cooper as a part of the crew to keep the beer casks tight and to repair damages to them occurring in heavy weather.

spring, bringing a supply of lemons, that the progress of the disease was checked.

The *Arbella* also carried fourteen tuns of drinking water (thirty-five hundred gallons), two hogsheads of 'syder,' and one hogshead of vinegar. This supply of fluids was their rations for twelve weeks. For solid food this ship carried sixteen hogsheads of meat, of which there was beef (eight thousand pounds), pork (twenty-eight hundred pounds), and a quantity of beef tongues. It cost them nineteen shillings per hundredweight for beef, and twenty shillings for pork. The tongues were priced at fourteen pence apiece. Of course, this meat was prepared for the voyage according to the art or 'mystery' of preserving meat practiced by the Salters Company. It was evidently a satisfactory delivery, for the Governor wrote home that the beef 'was as sweet and good as if it were but a month powdered.' In addition to this they had six hundred pounds of 'haberdyne' (salt codfish) and for good measure they had one barrel of salt and one hundred pounds of suet, presumably for cooking purposes. The staff of life was represented by twenty thousand biscuits, of which fifteen thousand were brown and five thousand white, supplemented by one barrel of flour, thirty bushels of oatmeal, and eleven firkins of butter as a spread. The only vegetable in their table of supplies was peas, of which they had forty bushels. These were dried peas. To make this unembellished diet palatable they provided the cook with a bushel and a half of mustard seed to stimulate their jaded appetites after days and weeks of 'salthorse.' [1] Of course, individual passengers brought small supplies of food for their own use, probably relishes to relieve the monotony of sea diet. As a result

[1] All these items of supplies are from notes found inside the covers of the manuscript Journal of Winthrop. The meat supply was bought of a butcher in East Cheap, London, and the bread of a baker in Southwark.

result of his own experience Winthrop wrote to his wife that when she came over the following year to bring a supply of 'pease that would porridge well.' He added one practical suggestion, doubtless the outgrowth of his own experiences: 'Be sure to have ready at sea 2: or 3: skillets of several syzes, a large fryinge panne, a small stewinge panne & a case to boyle a pudding in,' which implies that the passengers cooked some of their own meals, or parts of them. Evidently the Steward's department of the Fleet was not yet experienced or efficient in serving regular meals for so many people, satis-factorily.

Deep-sea fishing supplemented the larder, giving them fresh fish as the exigencies of the weather permitted and as luck favored their angling. As they approached the Grand Banks codfishing was always rewarded by plentiful catches. The galley was furnished with the following list of utensils and tableware:

The Cookes Store

100	platters	3½	duzen Musterd dishes
4	Trayes	2½	Duzen butter dishes
2	wooden bowlles	3	or 4 duzen Trenchers
4	Lanthornes	1	duzen Codd-lyne
4	pompes for water and beer	3	duzen Coddhookes
3½	duzen of quart cans	½	duzen Mackerell lynes
3	duzen of small cans	1½	duzen Mackerell hookes
13	duzen of Wooden Spoones	12	leades
3½	duzen Bread basketts	6	small Leades [1]

The following attractive suggestions were made by Wood re-garding luxuries 'for such as have ability... some conserves and good Clarret wine to burne at Sea: or you may have it by some of your Vintners or Wine Coopers burned here, and put up in Vessels.'

It

[1] *Ibid.*

It is evident that artificial lights were not supplied to passengers, and that sundown was the signal for retiring. This appears to be a logical conclusion from the fact that only four 'lanthornes' and six dozen candles were provided, and as far as ascertainable, the only heat on the vessel was from the cooking-stove in the galley, for which eight thousand of 'burneing wood' was carried. Their descendants, who now travel in our leviathans of the deep, surrounded by all the luxuries that embellish modern voyages, will have difficulty in visualizing this picture of conditions that existed three centuries ago.

CHAPTER V

The Voyage Overseas

AS soon as the agreement at Cambridge on August 26, 1629, was consummated, the Company began to arrange for shipping to carry the emigrants across the Atlantic. In the next month the ship *Eagle* (mounting twenty-eight guns and carrying a crew of fifty-two seamen) was bought for the Company's use by ten of the members as underwriters. This plan was in accordance with the suggestion of the Reverend Francis Higginson as a business proposition that it would be more economical for a party of emigrants to join together and purchase a ship for the voyage and dispose of it after arrival.[1] This ship was later christened the *Arbella* in honor of the Lady Arbella. The following additional ships were chartered during the year for service in the spring, viz.:

Ambrose	*Mayflower*	*Whale*
Jewel	*William and Francis*	*Success*
Talbot	*Hopewell*	*Trial*
Charles		

It was provided that the fleet should be 'Ready to set saile from London by the first day of March and that if any passengers bee to take shipp at Isle of Wight the ships shall stoppe there twenty-four hours.'[2] Presumably the usual delays

[1] Letter of the Reverend Francis Higginson in *Hutchinson Collection*, 48. The *Arbella*, which was purchased by a number of individuals in the Company and in turn was chartered by them to the Company for the voyage. The charter price was £750, a part of which was to be advanced and 'the rest upon Certificate of our safe Arivall.' (Unpublished Note in Winthrop's original Journal.) The *Ambrose* and *Jewel* were owned by Matthew Cradock.

[2] *M.C.R.*, 1, 65. Doubtless this provision for an embarkation point at Southampton was to enable the Governor and officials of the Company to attend to emergency
gency

delays prevented adherence to this schedule and the month of April arrived before the fleet had assembled at Southampton Water, the final rendezvous. A plan of consortship was arranged by which the *Arbella* was designated 'Admiral,' the *Talbot* 'Vice Admiral,' the *Ambrose* 'Rear Admiral,' and the *Jewel* a 'Captain' in nautical ranking for the fleet, and a code of signals was agreed upon for use at sea to maintain contact and regulate their movements. Winthrop went down to Southampton on the 10th of March to superintend the assembling of supplies and loading the ships, where he was held in suspense pending the arrival of the ships from London. It can be inferred from available records that only the four leaders of the Fleet, named above, carried passengers, as well as the *Mayflower*, *Whale*, and *Success*. The others were used to transport freight and live stock. These vessels began to drift in to The Solent between his arrival and the last of the month. From this point the sole authority on the voyage of this grand fleet — the greatest ever assembled to carry Englishmen overseas to a new homeland — is John Winthrop himself, who began his famous journal of the voyage under these headlines:

ANNO DOMINI 1630, MARCH 29 MONDAY

Easter Monday.   Ryding at the Cowes, near the Isle of Wight.

What follows this introductory entry in his log is a condensed narration of the principal events of interest which marked the progress of this famous flotilla to the shores of their Utopia.

On

gency business in London and to pick up any late applicants for transportation after the lists were closed and while the fleet was going down the Thames and into the English Channel. In addition supplies of fresh vegetables and water could be procured there. The trip from London to the Isle of Wight represented so much lost time and so many lost miles logged and diminution of food supplies.

On Tuesday, April 6, Matthew Cradock, the late Governor of the Massachusetts Bay Company, arrived from London to take his official leave of the party and when this formality was over and he was duly saluted as he went over the side, these four ships led by the *Arbella* weighed anchor and leisurely sailed down The Solent and came to anchorage before the castle at Yarmouth on the west end of the Isle of Wight. More salutes between the Castle and the Flagship.

It is necessary here to mention an historic event which for some reason is given no mention by Winthrop in his Journal or in his letters to his wife before sailing. Reference is made to the famous farewell address of the Reverend John Cotton, Vicar of Boston, Lincolnshire, who came down to give his blessing and approval of the undertaking, but where this address was delivered is uncertain, as two contemporary authorities place it at Gravesend and at Southampton. John Rous in his Diary of the year 1630 makes the following record:

> Some little while since, the Company went to New England under Mr. Wintrop. Mr. Cotton, of Boston in Lincolnshire, went to their departure about Gravesend & preached to them, as we heare, out of 2 Samuel, vii. 10.[1] It is said that he is prohibited for preaching any more in England then untill June 24 next now coming.[2]

Another who should be a competent authority, as a passenger in the Winthrop Fleet, places the scene of this sermon at Southampton. In a letter from Samuel Fuller of Plymouth to Governor Bradford, dated Charlestown, August 2, 1630, only three weeks after the arrival of the Fleet, he wrote:

Here

---

[1] 'Moreover I will appoint a place for my people Israel, and they will plant them, that they may dwell in a place of their own, and move no more; neither shall the children of wickedness afflict them any more, as beforetime.'

[2] Camden Society, LVI, 53, 54.

Here is a gentleman, one Mr. William Cottington, (a Boston Man), who tould me, that Mr. Cottons charge at Hamton was, that they should take advise of them at Plimoth, and should doe nothing to offend them.[1]

This farewell sermon was published by John Humfrey in the same year entitled 'God's Promise to his Plantation.'[2] The evidence favors Southampton as the scene of its delivery, but the silence of Winthrop is inexplicable. Nor does he mention the visits of friends and relatives coming to bid farewell to the departing emigrants, as Bradford and Winslow related the touching scenes when the Pilgrims left Delfthaven. Johnson, however, although not a participant, supplies material for this part of the story. He records that some of them 'had their speach strangled from the depth of their inward dolor with heart-breaking sobs... adding many drops of salt liquor to the ebbing ocean.' He could not refrain from adding that some of the idlers on the dock expressed the opinion that the participants in this emigration were 'cract-braines.'[3]

They stayed at anchor off the Castle of Yarmouth for a week, waiting for the seven vessels left behind at Southampton which were not yet ready for the long voyage. This week of idleness was made bearable for the godly by a fast on Friday, which some ungodly landmen improved by tapping a 'rundlet of strongwater' and making merry with the stolen cups of liquor. The culprits were laid in bolts all night, whipped in the morning, and dieted on bread and water the following day while sobering up. On Monday, April 6, the Captain of Yarmouth Castle, 'a grave, comely gentleman, and of great age,' came aboard the *Arbella* and

was

---

[1] Bradford: *History of Plimmoth Plantation* (Ford ed.), II, 115, 116.
[2] 3 *Mass. Hist. Soc. Proc.*, XLI, 101; XLIII, 503.
[3] *Wonder-Working Providence.*

was entertained at breakfast. He had sailed on the seven seas in Elizabeth's reign, had been in a Spanish prison for three years, and with his three sons was on the famous voyage to Guiana in 1610 under Sir Thomas Roe. Doubtless this typical old British salt regaled them with his experiences on the Atlantic and, in his honor as he was piped down the side, four shots from the forecastle waked echoes on The Solent.

Again Mr. Cradock came aboard to announce that the rest of the fleet had dropped down to Stokes Bay opposite Cowes and would sail by St. Helen's Point (now Bembridge Foreland) into the Channel and at last all was ready — or nearly so. The Governor's son Henry and Mr. Pelham, who went off to attend to shipping the cattle, were left behind to join some later ship. On Thursday, April 8, at six in the morning, the 'Admiral' weighed anchor and set sail, followed by her three consorts in scattered formation. Accompanying them were some small ships bound for New Foundland. The rest of the seven vessels of the fleet were not ready until two or three weeks later, but as there is no known existing record of their experiences in crossing the ocean the story of the Fleet only applies to the 'Admiral' and her consorts. The others were not heard from until their safe arrival on the New England coast. By ten in the forenoon of the first day they were past the Needles and at daylight on Friday the 9th the Bill of Portland was abeam the flagship *Arbella* and the first excitement of the trip is described by Winthrop, when decks were cleared for action against a suspected enemy fleet:

> In the morning we descried from the top eight sail astern of us, (whom Capt. Lowe told us he had seen at Dunnose in the evening). We supposing they might be Dunkirkers, our captain caused the gunroom and gundeck to be cleared; all the hammocks were taken down, our ordnance loaded, and our
> powder-chests

powder-chests and fireworks made ready, and our landmen quartered among the seamen, and twenty-five of them appointed for muskets, and every man written down for his quarter.

The wind continued N. [blank] with fair weather, and afternoon it calmed, and we still saw those eight ships to stand towards us; having more wind than we, they came up apace, so as our captain and the masters of our consorts were more occasioned to think they might be Dunkirkers,[1] (for we were told at Yarmouth, that there were ten sail of them waiting for us;) whereupon we all prepared to fight with them, and took down some cabins which were in the way of our ordnance, and out of every ship were thrown such bed matters as were subject to take fire, and we heaved out our long boats, and put up our waste cloths, and drew forth our men, and armed them with muskets and other weapons, and instruments for fireworks; and for an experiment our captain shot a ball of wild-fire fastened to an arrow out of a cross-bow, which burnt in the water a good time. The lady Arbella and the other women and children were removed into the lower deck, that they might be out of danger. All things being thus fitted, we went to prayer upon the upper deck. It was much to see how cheerful and comfortable all the company appeared; not a woman or child that showed fear, though all did apprehend the danger to have been great, if things had proved as might well be expected, for there had been eight against four, and the least of the enemy's ships were reported to carry thirty brass pieces; but our trust was in the Lord of Hosts; and the courage of our captain, and his care and diligence, did much to encourage us. It was now about one of the clock, and the fleet seemed to be within a league of us; therefore our captain, because he would show he was not afraid of them, and that he might see the issue before night should overtake us, tacked about and stood to meet them, and when we came near we perceived them to be our friends, — the Little Neptune, a ship of some twenty pieces of ordnance and her two consorts, bound for the Straits; a ship of Flushing, and a Frenchman, and three other English ships bound for Canada and Newfoundland. So when we drew near, every ship

[1] Dunkirk was then a possession of Spain, at that time at war with England.

ship (as they met) saluted each other, and the musketeers dis-
charged their small shot; and so (God be praised) our fear and
danger was turned into mirth and friendly entertainment.
Our danger being thus over, we espied two boats on fishing in
the channel; so every of our four ships manned out a skiff, and
we bought of them great store of excellent fresh fish of divers
sorts.

This thrilling description of a naval engagement that
almost happened discloses some facts which lets light upon
the method of providing 'accommodations' for passengers
on overseas travel. It has been explained that vessels of this
fleet were ordinary freighters, built for transporting merchandise, dry and wet goods, from Mediterranean and European ports to and from English ports. The carrying of passengers on voyages lasting two or three months was never in
the plans of shipbuilders or merchant adventurers of that era.
Only naval vessels were constructed with this end in view
and the coastwise craft chartered for the Atlantic voyages
were ill-fitted to afford the necessary comforts for women
and children. Temporary, makeshift 'cabins' between decks
were installed on them for protection from the elements and
privacy in the night watches.

When peace again settled over this much worried flotilla
the voyage was resumed and by Saturday morning they
were 'over against' Plymouth and later in the day the Lizard
hove in sight. The Scilly Isles were passed the next morning
(Sunday the 11th) and now, out of the English Channel,
ahead of them lay the great ocean with nearly three thousand
miles to be traversed before they would sight land again.
The inevitable conditions ensued as the little vessels headed
into the unending swells and choppy seas of the Atlantic
and they began to toss over its surface, churned under a
'very stiff gale' from the Northwest. Everybody was too
seasick,

seasick, both minister and people, and the usual religious services on their first Sabbath at sea were omitted. This temporary difficulty, 'which put us all out of order,' says Winthrop, lasted for a day or more, and the method employed to restore their drooping spirits and uncertain stomachs is related by him:

> Our children and others, that were sick, and lay groaning in the cabins, we fetched out, and having stretched a rope from the steerage to the mainmast, we made them stand, some of one side and some of the other, and sway it up and down till they were warm, and by this means they soon grew well and merry.

Having become enured to the novel equilibrium of the unstable decks, this inevitable feature of the voyage soon became negligible and the usual routine was resumed. On the next Sunday at sea religious services were held on the ships, and even in stormy weather, and on week days prayer meetings were held. Catechizing of the children was done on Tuesdays and Wednesdays.

It will not be interesting nor important to recite the daily progress of the fleet, or the variations in the weather during the long weeks on the ocean. The temperature for the first half of the voyage was generally low and so cold 'as we could well endure our warmer clothes.'[1] The first comfortably warm day was on April 26, as noted by Winthrop, two weeks out, but it was only of short duration. Gales called by him 'stiff,' 'pretty,' or 'handsome' followed each other with seas 'high' or 'raging' in regular succession. On May 3 they were obliged to 'lay at hull,' so great was the stress of the stormy seas, and heavy rains generally accompanied these conditions.

---

[1] From his experience Winthrop was able to send his wife injunctions on this necessity. 'Be sure,' he wrote her, 'to be warm clothed... and to bring a store of linnen for use at sea.'

tions. On May 19 they had reached (or thought they had) the Grand Banks in the midst of a great storm, and at nine of the clock at night a fast was observed and again the following day. Some of the vessels lost their smaller sails at this time as the storm continued with little abatement for several days. Scarcely any headway was made during this prolonged bad weather. The live stock, which was carried in separate ships, suffered as much, if not more than the passengers, as they were helpless on the storm-swept decks. There were two hundred and forty cows and about sixty horses transported with the Fleet, according to Winthrop. Captain John Smith, describing this storm, which lasted ten days, stated that the cattle 'were so tossed and brused, three score and ten died.' [1]

The nautical devices used by Captain Milborne of the *Arbella* to bring his ship to its destined port were the crude methods available at that period. Navigators had only the cross-staff to ascertain the latitude, but while the elevation of the sun could be measured with practical accuracy by this instrument and the degrees of latitude figured out there was no way to determine longitude at sea. This requirement was not available for mariners until the latter half of the next century. To overcome this difficulty, the east or west positions at a given time were expressed in terms of dead reckoning by estimating the marine leagues sailed from day to day. As they progressed west, Winthrop enters in his Journal such statements as 'about 90 leagues from Scilly.'

It was evidently the plan of the navigator of the *Arbella* as Admiral of the Fleet to use latitude 43° 15' north as his general westerly course, which would bring him directly south of Cape Sable, Nova Scotia, and to the Isles of Shoals. The *Arbella* reached this latitude on May 3rd when just north of Terceira,

[1] *Advertisement for Planters.*

Terceira, Azores, and he varied little from this course except when driven from it, above or below, by stress of weather. When he reached the Gulf of Maine and came in permanent view of the coast of New England his course was determined by well-known landmarks.

On May 30 they reckoned they were on the meridian of Cape Sable but soundings gave no 'ground' at about eighty fathoms, and on June 6 they sighted land 'about five or six leagues off' and on the following day (Monday, 7th) found they were in thirty fathoms with a calmer sea. 'So we put our ship a-stays,' writes Winthrop, 'and took in less than two hours, with a few hooks, sixty-seven codfish, most of them very great fish, some a yard and a half long and a yard in compass.' While these incidents of the voyage of a material character were being enacted, Winthrop found time in the seclusion of the cabin to employ his busy pen in setting down some of his religious convictions. He wrote an essay which he entitled 'A Model of Christian Charity,' the original of which is still in existence.

The scent of the nearing coast-line was now more and more in evidence and on June 9, with a 'handsome gale' to speed them on, they 'had the mainland upon our starboard all day' and saw 'very high land' and 'many small islands' off the coast of Maine. The worst of this stormy crossing was now nearly over. On June 10 they made the Three Turks Heads on their starboard bow, meaning the three peaks of Mount Agamenticus in York, Maine; then Boone Island and the 'Shoals' assured them that the end of the voyage was at hand.

These were the externals which the leaders of the Fleet had encountered in the past sixty-eight cold and stormy days and nights. What of the human beings tossed on the bosom of the ocean toward the unknown shores of New England, and how

how did they fare? That they suffered hardships needs no recital. Death continually hovered in the wake of the flotilla and we are told that many of the passengers of the *Success* were nearly starved when they reached their destination. Yet during the voyage, when weather and sea conditions permitted, there was occasional visiting between the ships and dinner parties were held for the men 'in the round house' (meaning the Master's cabin) of the *Arbella*,[1] and the ladies were served in the 'great cabin' on these festal occasions. A squadron under command of Captain Thomas Kirk, bound for Quebec, was overtaken and while in their company like social courtesies followed. Exchanges of food between vessels was made to equalize the supplies whenever possible, but the commissariat was not equal to the requirements of a balanced dietary. They were ignorant of its principles.

Winthrop notes that a swallow lighted on his ship when ninety miles from Scilly and again when off Nova Scotia 'a wild pigeon and a small land bird' flew aboard as harbingers of the nearing coast. He noted that the new moon in April and May looked much smaller than the moons in England, and on May 31 he writes, 'this day about five at night we expected the eclipse,' but for some reason this celestial phenomenon did not perform. An eclipse was due at this date, but probably due to inability to reckon the time accurately and perhaps from obscuration by clouds it was invisible to the Fleet. It was a total solar eclipse which would have been visible in England. About halfway across they saw a whale who lay 'just in our ship's way (the bunch of his back about a yard above water). He would not shun us; so we passed within a stone's cast of him, as he lay spouting up water.'

Winthrop speaks on three occasions of the 'landsmen' and
once

---

[1] *Seaman's Grammar* (1627), ii, 6; Smith: *Accidence for Young Seamen*, 10. It was the 'utmost' cabin in the overhanging stern.

once of the 'musketeers.' In nautical terms a landsman is a sailor on his first voyage, and it appears that they were assigned to the duty of soldiers or guardsmen and drilled in the use of muskets for defensive purposes. It is known that two professional military men — Captain John Underhill and Captain Daniel Patrick — were employed to act as leaders in military operations after arrival in New England. It is probable that they had duties of this character during the voyage should any emergency like the one recited in the beginning of this chapter arise. They followed in this matter the example of the Pilgrims in the employment of Captain Myles Standish for the same purpose.

Deaths occurred as a not unexpected event in such a large party living under unfavorable conditions; one of them a seaman, 'a profane fellow' according to the journalist. The *Talbot* lost fourteen passengers by death on the voyage, an impressive record on a small ship. A child was born on the *Jewel* and one woman on the *Arbella* was brought to bed of a still-born infant.

At last on June 12, land came to be a reality to the sight of the tired voyagers, when they reached Cape Ann; and those who were able went ashore and 'gathered a store of fine strawberries.' The next day (Sunday), Miasconomo, the Sagamore of Agawam, came aboard and presumably welcomed the strangers to the home of his forefathers. At all events he stayed all day. Festivities continued with visits from the Masters of vessels already in the harbor of Salem, while the Governor and the Assistants, with some of the women, went to the residence of Captain Endicott and enjoyed a real meal in which venison pasty and good beer tempted their jaded appetites. On Wednesday the 18th, the *Jewel* having been the second vessel of the Fleet to reach port, all disembarked and the Promised Land lay at their feet.

feet. The *Mayflower* and *Whale* dropped anchor in Charlestown Harbor two weeks later, July 1, followed by the *Talbot* the next day. The *William and Francis* and *Hopewell* arrived the 3d, the *Trial* and the *Charles* the 5th, and the 6th of July saw the *Success*, the last of the Fleet, safely at anchor in Salem Harbor.[1] The Great Emigration had reached its destination. With their faces looking back to the East, whence they had wearily sailed a thousand leagues, cradled in Atlantic tempests, they could say then with the Evangelist:

'And there shall be no more Sea.'

[1] It may be noted that Winthrop does not record any service of thanks for their safe arrival, such as so impressively stated by Bradford when the Pilgrims of the *Mayflower* ended their long voyage in safety. It can be stated here that Winthrop wrote another 'Journal and Relation' of the voyage which he sent to his brother-in-law Emanuel Downing. He asked his son John Winthrop, Jr., to send a copy of it to Sir Nathaniel Barnardiston, a prominent Puritan sympathizer (*Life and Letters of John Winthrop*, II, 41).

CHAPTER VI

The Passengers and their Origins

PROBABLY few of those who participated in this great movement had any conception that their names would be eagerly sought three centuries later for a permanent record in the annals of the nation they were destined to establish. The story of an event which became of historic importance is only half told if the identity of the participants is not revealed, for it is the natural impulse of man to confer even posthumous honors on the men and women who took part in it. So it will be asked who were these adventurous souls who sailed three thousand miles to our shores in craft so frail and so absurdly small that no one of their descendants could be induced to risk its perils to-day? It is essential to the completeness of the story to know them by name, for this voyage was the beginning of the greatest movement in American colonization. To answer this it will be necessary to know how many emigrants sailed in this flotilla before a list can be compiled with any surety of completeness. Fortunately, Winthrop, in a letter to his wife written just before sailing, told her that there were seven hundred passengers aboard.[1] While this statement needs no corroboration, yet it is satisfactory to have a contemporary writer give independent testimony that 'six or seven hundred went with him.'[2] A much larger number has been claimed by later historians, but no authority for their figures has been given nor any reason offered for ignoring Winthrop's specific statement.[3]

Therefore,

---

[1] *Life and Letters of John Winthrop*, 1, 378.

[2] John Smith: *Advertisement for Planters.*

[3] Palfrey, *History of New England*, gives the number as eight hundred and forty (1, 313), and Adams, *Founding of New England*, states that there were 'between nine

Therefore, we have to deal with about seven hundred men, women, and children as embarked for the adventure and then subtract the casualties of the voyage, deaths that ensued shortly after arrival from disease, the return of discontented persons, and the few who came as prospectors to view the country and examine its desirability for planting a colony. On these points we have a detailed statement written six months after their arrival by Thomas Dudley to Bridget, Countess of Lincoln, mother of the Lady Arbella. It was sent back by the *Lyon* April 1, 1631, and reached England in four weeks.[1] He wrote her that from the time they weighed anchor in April, 1630, to the following December, 'there dyed by estimacon about two hundred at least, so lowe hath the Lord brought us.' On the score of desertions — return of the discontented — he gives these details:

... Insomuch that the shippes being now uppon their returne, some for England, some for Ireland, there was I take it, not much less than an hundred, (some think many more) partly out of dislike of our government, which restrained and punished their excesses, and partly through fear of famine, (not seeing other means than by their labour to feed themselves) which returned back again. And glad were wee to bee ridd of them. Others also afterwards hearing of men of their own disposition, which were planted at Piscataway, went from us to them, whereby though our numbers were lessened, yet wee accounted ourselves nothing weakened by their removall....'[2]

Thus from Dudley's account there must be subtracted two hundred

nine hundred and a thousand' (1, 140). Palfrey added the one hundred and forty who came in the *Mary and John* from Plymouth, a separate company from the 'West Country' under the patronage of the Reverend John White.

[1] Young: *Chronicles of Massachusetts.*

[2] *Ibid.* It has not been possible to make a satisfactory identification of those who are said to have gone to the Piscataqua (New Hampshire), region, except Colonel Walter Norton, and Edward Johnson who settled in York, and Thomas Walford who went to Portsmouth, but they were of the 'Old Planters' group.

hundred deaths and about one hundred desertions or removals from the seven hundred who set sail in April, 1630, and the remaining four hundred and fifty appear to be the number of passengers to be accounted for by name, as no record of the deaths occurring at sea or after arrival is extant. We only know of a few of the more prominent persons like Isaac Johnson and his wife, the Lady Arbella, the wives of the Reverend George Phillips and Mr. William Pynchon, and the accidental drowning of young Henry Winthrop. The deaths of thirty-five others are found in various sources, leaving one hundred and sixty-five casualties unaccounted for, probably 'the poorer sort' mentioned by Winthrop. Of the hundred who removed to adjoining settlements or returned to England but twenty-seven are known by name.

It is more than probable that the number of deaths and removals were estimated by Dudley and stated in 'round numbers.' He must have included the casualties of the Dorchester settlers who came in the *Mary and John*, as well as those of the *Lyon*, and would be likely to exaggerate the desertion of undesirables, of whom they were glad 'to bee ridd.' The inference drawn would show the remaining settlers classified as 'godly persons.' These totals make up the seven hundred passengers.

Fortunately, for our purposes, there exists a list of seventy names of those who came with the fleet, a rough list prepared by Winthrop, and to be found entered on a flyleaf in the original Winthrop Journal disconnected with the main text. A facsimile of this important record appears herewith. As this list comprises only males the names of women and children accompanying them, as well as the other emigrants not recorded by Winthrop, must be sifted out of many existing records, Colonial, Town, church, and family papers, and be differentiated from the older planters who were settled at Charlestown,

Charlestown, Dorchester, Salem, and adjacent places in the Bay before the arrival of the Winthrop Fleet. This is not always easy of accomplishment and in many cases it required a search in England to determine whether a particular settler of 1630 came with the *Mary and John* from Plymouth, with Endicott in 1628, or by other vessels individually. The first list of persons requesting to be made freemen on October 19, 1630, contains the names of Old Planters of Charlestown and Salem, as well as the Dorchester party from the West Country mingled with those of the Winthrop Fleet, so that it gives no definite clue to the passengers of the latter named vessels.[1] This list contains one hundred and nine names and on May 18, 1631, there were one hundred and fourteen persons made freemen.[2] With few exceptions they were the men who had applied for the franchise the preceding October, so this list does not solve the problem. The next source of identification is the list of members of the First Church of Boston at its foundation in Charlestown, 1630, and subsequent admissions during a number of succeeding years, as some who are positively known to have come with this Fleet did not join the church for several years.[3] Many of them did not become affiliated with the church at all, and many did not join at its founding, which is ample proof that they did not emigrate for religious reasons. The church list therefore is not a safe source of authority as to the problem. In the final justification for the inclusion of a name, other than the few who are mentioned specifically as coming in the Fleet, the decision must rest on identification of the individual in his English home, and where that is impossible, all the circumstantial factors entering in each case must be weighed. The surname is important, whether East Anglian or West Country;

[1] *Mass. Col. Rec.*, I, 79, 80.   [2] *Ibid.*, I, 366.
[3] Hill: *History of the First Church, Boston.*

Country; the passenger's kinsfolk and associates; his neighbors in the town where he settled, and the weight of evidence for and against his origin in that part of England whence the great bulk of the passengers of the Winthrop Fleet originated, these are some of the constituent elements of the problems which entered into the composition of the passenger list of those who can be assumed or proven to have come with Winthrop.

Whence came this company of voyagers seeking a new home in a trackless wilderness? The news of their coming had already reached our shores. The Reverend Francis Higginson at Salem, who had preceded them hither by a year, wrote to some of his old friends in Leicestershire under date of 24 July, 1629, that 'a great company of godly Christians out of London' were expected next year (1630),[1] and Thomas Prince, a later historian, in speaking of the Migration, said, 'the greatest Number came from About *London* tho' *South Hampton* was the place of Rendevouz.'[2] While it is true that many came 'out of London' and 'about London' it is not true that the majority of them originated in that city. As has been stated, there were many foci of activities in spreading the gospel of emigration to New England both before and after Winthrop assumed active control of the movement. Analysis of the home origins of the passengers as compiled by the author shows that they came from twenty different counties of England in the following relative order:

Suffolk	159	Kent	5
Essex	92	Lancashire	5
London	78	Hampshire	5
Northamptonshire	22	Norfolk	4
Lincolnshire	12	Oxfordshire	3
Yorkshire	8	Buckinghamshire	2
Leicestershire	7	Hertfordshire	2

To

[1] Hutchinson Collection, 47.   [2] *New England Chronology* (1728), 211.

To this list are to be added Nottinghamshire, Cambridge-shire, Rutlandshire, and Chester with one each and five from Holland. This tabulation of origins, four hundred and more in number, does not give us a definite picture of the situation, as England is a small country and its forty small counties are so grouped that the comital lines make only an artificial boundary. This will be best shown on the accompanying map which represents county groupings that explain the restricted density of origins.

The Lincolnshire group can be attributed to the influence of the Reverend John Cotton, the Reverend Samuel Skelton, and the Fiennes family; the Leicestershire group to the Reverend Arthur Hildersham of Ashby-de-la-Zouch and the Reverend Francis Higginson; the Northamptonshire group to Thomas Dudley and the Reverend Samuel Stone; the Lancashire group probably to the Reverend Richard Mather, and the large London group to the numerous dissenting clergymen in the city parishes as well as to the business in-fluence of the lay members of the Company residing there. Of course, Winthrop can be personally credited as an im-portant factor in his own county. Using as a center Groton, of which he was Lord of the Manor, about a hundred persons came from surrounding parishes within a radius of ten miles. Most of the adjoining county of Essex was then under the spell of the Reverend Thomas Hooker, Hugh Peter, and John Eliot, preaching and teaching in and around Chelms-ford, while William Pynchon, of the old landed gentry in Writtle near by, gave the movement its business aspect in that county.

Of the social qualities of these passengers there are certain facts which permit some definite statements as to their status in the domestic life of the mother country. Lady Arbella Fiennes, daughter of an earl, and her brother Charles carried
the

the honors of nobility for the passengers, while Sir Richard Saltonstall, knight, was the sole representative of the titled gentry. Next in rank were Isaac Johnson and John Winthrop, both esquires. Brand, Feake, Plaistow, and Pynchon were of the 'gentleman' class, and following them were the undefined persons who for one reason or another were given the prefix of 'Mr.' in our early records: Alcock, Bradstreet, Browne, Coddington, Cole, Dillingham, Dudley, Freeman, Glover, Jones, Masters, Mayhew, Pelham, Stoughton, Turner, Tyndale, and Vassall. Thus twenty-five of the two hundred and forty-seven possible heads of families were of a social rank above that of yeomen or husbandmen. The great majority of the passengers were artisans or tillers of the soil who were called 'planters' — not in the agricultural sense, but as persons who were engaged in planting a colony under the flag of England. Of the trades represented, as far as known, there were the following, viz.: armorer, baker, blacksmith, butcher, carpenter, cordwainer, merchant, five of each; clothier, chandler, cooper, military officer, physician, tailor, three each; fisherman, herdsman, mason, two each; tanner and weaver, one each. This list is, of course, incomplete, but recites the known or recorded vocations of the passengers. 'These ships,' said Prince, 'were filled with Passengers of all occupations skill'd in all Kinds of Faculties needful for Planting a new Colony.' And an earlier writer, after stating that there were 'divers good and godly people' among them probably covered the situation fully by adding that 'people of all sorts went.'

From this list the following analysis of the classes of passengers can be deduced: there were two hundred and forty-three adult males, potential heads of families, but only one hundred and twenty-nine of them are known to have been accompanied by their wives and thus there were the same
number

number of married women in the passenger list. Thirteen single women or widows are of record as surviving the ordeal of the voyage and diseases in the first year. There were about one hundred and thirty-five children accompanying their parents and seventeen classed as servants. Three of the prominent leaders — Winthrop himself, Sir Richard Saltonstall, and the Reverend John Wilson — did not bring their wives with them, probably for the reason that they wished to prepare suitable homes for them in advance of their coming. It is further possible that most of the unattached females, presumed to be single, may have been widows of deceased passengers, or kinswomen of other families, as unmarried women did not travel alone on an adventure of this nature at that period.

Many inquiries have been received by the author, since the announcement of the issue of this volume, seeking information as to the names of the passengers of the *Arbella*. As there is no known list of the emigrants who came in the Winthrop Fleet, so there is none of those who came in particular ships, beyond the Governor himself, his three boys, and three other persons casually mentioned by him in his log of the voyage. In the Public Record Office, London, among the Colonial Papers,[1] there is a document, in the nature of a 'news' report, which gives the following names as having sailed recently for New England:

Mr. John Winthroppe Esqr. Governor and three of his sonnes
Sir Rich. Saltonstall Knight three of his sonnes and 2 daughters
Mr. Isaake Johnson Esqr and the Lady Arbella his wife sister to the Earle of Lincolne
Mr. Charles Fines the said Earles brother
Mr. Dudley his wife 2 sonnes and 4 daughters
Mr. Coddington and his wife

Mr.

[1] V, 75.

Mr. Pinchon and his wife and 3 daughters
Mr. Vassall and his wife
Mr. Revell

In view of the fact that social position and official connection with the company would give the above-named persons quarters on the flagship, it may be assumed, for these reasons and the convenience of conferences on business connected with their future settlement, that they came on the *Arbella*. The only objection to accepting this natural conclusion definitely is the fact that Mr. John Revell, who was an Assistant, was a passenger in the *Jewel*.[1]

With these explanations there will follow the names of those who are believed to have come to New England with Winthrop on the evidence cited in each individual case.

[1] Winthrop, *Journal*, I, 44.

Appendix

APPENDIX A

ALPHABETICAL LIST OF PASSENGERS

Key to Abbreviations

Savage	Genealogical Dictionary
M.C.R.	Mass. Colonial Records
Pope	Pioneers of Massachusetts
Winthrop	Journal of John Winthrop
G.R.	N.E. Genealogical Register
Winthrop MSS.	Collections Mass. Hist. Soc.
Bond	History of Watertown
Dudley Letter	To Countess of Lincoln 1631
B.T.R.	Boston Town Record
Waters & Emmerton	English Gleanings
L. & L. W.	Life & Letters John Winthrop
Lechford	Notarial Records
Banks MSS.	Collections of the Author
Ch.Ch.Rec.	Charlestown Church Records
Lechford P.D.	Lechford Plaine Dealing
P.C.C.	Prerogative Court of Canterbury
Sewall	Diary of Samuel Sewall
Eliot	Roxbury Church Records
G.L.	Plans of Boston, 1905, by George Lamb

ABBOTT, DANIEL
Cambridge

Juror, 18 Sept. 1630 (M.C.R., I, 78). Freeman 18 May 1631 (*ibid.*, I, 366). Removed to Providence before 1639.

ABELL, ROBERT
Boston

From Hemington, Leicestershire (P.C.C., 10 St. John). Applied freeman 19 Oct. 1630 (M.C.R., I, 80). Freeman 18 May 1631 (*ibid.*, I, 366). Related to the Cotton family and probably emigrated under influence of Rev. John Cotton or Rev. Arthur Hildersham of Ashby-de-la-Zouch, who lived a few miles from the home of Abell. Derby, the home of the Cotton family, was only five miles distant. Removed to Weymouth and later to Rehoboth.

AGAR, WILLIAM

AGAR, WILLIAM *Watertown*	Probably from Nazing Essex, or vicinity. An Agar family lived in Nazing, and the mother of Rev. John Eliot was named Lettice Aggar or Agar. William Agar was made a Freeman 18 May 1631 (M.C.R., I, 366). He died in 1684.
ALCOCK, GEORGE *Roxbury*	Probably from Leicestershire. Applied freeman 19 Oct. 1630 (M.C.R., I, 80). Freeman 18 May 1631 (*ibid.* 366). Deputy to General Court. Died December 1640.
ALCOCK, ——	Wife of George. Died 1630. She was sister of Rev. Thos. Hooker (Dudley Letter).
ALCOCK, THOMAS *Boston*	Brother of George. Probably from Leicestershire. Member church 1630/1, No. 46. Removed to Dedham (Pope). Freeman 6 May 1635 (M.C.R., I, 370). Died 1657 (G.R., IX, 344).
ALEWORTH, FRANCIS	Ordered to be sent back by the *Lyon* in March 1631, as undesirable (M.C.R., I, 82), but in July he was chosen Lieutenant.
ANDREW, THOMAS *Watertown*	Probably from Essex (Servant of Josiah Plaistow). Before court 27 Sept. 1631 (M.C.R., I, 92).
ARCHER, SAMUEL *Salem*	Applied freeman 19 Oct. 1630 (M.C.R., I, 80). Carpenter. Deposed 1660 aged 52 (b. 1608). Deposed 1667 aged 58 (b. 1609).
ASPINWALL, WILLIAM *Boston*	Came from Manchester, Lancashire. Notary public. Deacon 1630. Applied freeman 19 Oct. 1630 (M.C.R., I, 79). Member church, No. 10. Freeman 3 April 1632 (M.C.R., I, 367). Returned to England and died there.
Aspinwall, Elizabeth Aspinwall, Edward	Wife of William. Member church, No. 16. Son of William. Born 1630, just after arrival.
AUDLEY, (ODLIN) JOHN *Boston*	Probably from London. Member church 1630, No. 139. 'One of the very first inhabitants

habitants of Boston' (Sewall), but he was not a freeman until 1634. Armorer and cutler. Died 1685, aged 82 years (G.R., VI, 727).

BAKER, JOHN
Charlestown
Baker, Charity

No. 12 on first list of inhabitants. Freeman 3 March 1634 (Pope, 28; M.C.R., I, 75). Wife of John. Admitted church 1630 (Ch. Ch.Rec.).

BALSTON, WILLIAM
Boston

'Bolson' in Winthrop's list, possibly variant of Boylston. London is probable origin, but name common in Dorset and Somerset. Applied freeman 19 Oct. 1630 (M.C.R., I, 80); juror 1630 (*ibid.*, 81); removed to Rhode Island 1638 on account of connection with Mrs. Hutchinson's supporters.

Balston, Elizabeth

Wife of William. Died 'soon.' Admitted church 1630, No. 39.

BARSHAM, WILLIAM
Watertown

Juror 1630 (M.C.R., I, 78). Died 3 July 1684. Wife Annabel (Bland). Origin undetermined, but name is common in Norfolk.

BARTLETT, THOMAS
Watertown

Servant to Mr. Pelham 1631. Died 26 April 1654, aged 60 (b. 1594). Probably from Essex (M.C.R., I, 86).

BATEMAN, WILLIAM
Charlestown

From London. Freeman 18 May 1631. Died 16 Sept. 1631 (M.C.R., I, 78).

BAXTER, GREGORY
Roxbury

Perhaps from Sporle, co. Norfolk. Freeman 6 March 1631/2 (M.C.R., I, 367). Member church 1631/2.

BEAMSLEY, WILLIAM
Boston

Origin undetermined, but name found only in Lincoln, Lincolnshire. Probably came as servant and is called 'laborer' when admitted to church, 5 April, 1635. Freeman 25 May 1636 (M.C.R., I, 372). He died 1658.

Beamsley, Anne

Wife of William. Died about 1643 (B.T.R.).

BEECHER, THOMAS

BEECHER, THOMAS *Charlestown*	Came from Stepney. Mariner, master of *Talbot*. Member church 1631, No. 112. Died before 29(5) 1637 (Pope).
Beecher, Christian	Wife of Capt. Thomas. Member church 1630, No. 17. Daughter of James and Christian Barker of Harwich; married at Whitechapel (Pope).
BELCHER, EDWARD *Boston*	From Guilsborough, co. Northants. Member church 1630. Freeman 18 May 1631 (M.C.R., I, 366). Pipestave culler; soap boiler.
Belcher, Christian	Wife of Edward (Pope).
Belcher, Edward, Jr.	Son of Edward.
BENDALL, EDWARD *Boston*	From Southwark, co. Surrey. Merchant. Member church No. 77, 1630/1. Freeman 14 May 1634 (M.C.R., I, 369). Dismissed to a church in London 1653 (Pope).
Bendall, Anne	Wife of Edward. Died 25 (10) 1637 (Pope).
BENHAM, JOHN *Dorchester*	Origin unknown. Freeman 18 May 1631 (M.C.R., I, 80). Probably removed to New Haven.
BIGGS, JOHN *Boston*	From Groton, co. Suffolk, or vicinity. Member church No. 97, 1630/1. Freeman 4 March 1633/4 (M.C.R., I, 368). Ipswich 1633. Mentioned in letter of Bluette of Groton, Suffolk (Winthrop MSS.).
Biggs, Mary	Wife of John. Died 10 (11) 1649/50.
BLACK, JOHN *Charlestown*	Origin undetermined. Freeman March 1631/2. Admitted church 4 (11) 1634/5. Removed to Salem (Pope).
BOGGUST, JOHN	Probably from Boxted, Essex. John Boggus of Boxted had sons Robert and William. He was before court Sept. 1630 (M.C.R., I. 77).
BOSWELL, JOHN *Boston*	From London. Member church No. 94, 1630/1. Dead soon.

BOSWORTH, ZACCHEUS

BOSWORTH, ZACCHEUS
Boston

From Stowe IX Churches, co. Northants. Member church No. 98, 1630/1. Freeman 25 May 1636 (M.C.R., I, 372). Died 28 (5) 1655.

BOURNE, GARRET
Boston

Origin undetermined; lived on Boston Neck (G.L.). Freeman 6 May 1635 (M.C.R., I, 370). Removed to Rhode Island.

BOWMAN, NATHANIEL
Watertown

Applied freeman 19 Oct. 1630 (M.C.R., I, 80). At Cambridge 1650. Died 26 January 1681/2.

Bowman, Anna

Wife of Nathaniel.

BRADSTREET, SIMON
Cambridge

Born at Horbling, co. Lincoln, March 1603 (adjoining Sempringham). Probably associated with Earl of Lincoln. Married Anne Dudley, daughter of Thomas (M.C.R., I, 73).

Bradstreet, Anne

Wife of Simon. Born 1612; died 1672 (Pope).

BRAND, BENJAMIN
Boston

Applied freeman 19 Oct. 1630 (M.C.R., I, 79). Probably from Edwardston or Polstead, co. Suffolk (P.C.C., 81 Savill) will of Benjamin Brand, gent. of Edwardston 1621. Probably returned or died.

BRATCHER, AUGUSTINE
Charlestown

(Probably Bradshaw.) Origin unknown. Killed 1630. Inquest 28 Sept. 1630 (M.C.R., I, 77). He was a servant of Matthew Cradock.

BREASE, ——

Probably from Edwardston, Suffolk; called son-in-law of Mr. Huggins, a family living in E., and his 'tools' were to be sent to London before sailing (L. & L.W.). No further record; probably died early.

BRENTON, WILLIAM
Boston

Merchant. From Hammersmith, co. Middlesex (Savage). Admitted church Oct. 1633. Freeman 14 May 1634 (M.C.R., I, 369). Removed to Providence, R.I., where he died 1673/4 (G.L.).

BRETT, ISABEL

BRETT, ISABEL	Member church 1630/1, No. 88. 'Gone to Salem' (Boston Church Record).
BRIGHT, HENRY *Watertown*	From Bury St. Edmunds, Suffolk. Born 1580, aged 80 in 1660. Member church 1630/1, No. 48.
BROWNE, ABRAHAM *Watertown* Browne, Lydia	From Hawkdon, Suffolk (Bond). Freeman March 1631/2 (M.C.R., I, 367). Died 1650. Wife of Abraham. They had two children before 1632 (Pope).
BROWNE, JAMES *Boston*	Origin undetermined owing to commonness of name. Member church 1630, No. 61. Freeman 3 Sept. 1634 (M.C.R., I, 78).
BROWNE, RICHARD *Watertown*	From Hawkdon, Suffolk. Freeman 18 May 1631 (M.C.R., I, 366). Aged 81/2 in 1657 (b. 1575/6) (Bond). He probably came directly from London, where he 'kept a wherry,' and was a 'ruler' in one of the Separatist conventicles of the city (Hubbard).
Browne, Elizabeth Browne, George Browne, Richard, Jr.	Wife of Richard. Son of Richard. Returned to England (Bond). Son of Richard. Returned to England (Bond).
BUCKLAND, WILLIAM *Boston*	From Essex. Servant of Josiah Plaistow. Probably same as the Hingham carpenter. Removed to Rehoboth. Living 1661 (Winthrop).
BUGBY, RICHARD *Roxbury* Bugby, Judith	Perhaps S. John Hackney, Middlesex. Applied freeman 19 Oct. 1630 (M.C.R., I, 80). Freeman 18 May 1631 (M.C.R., I, 366). Died before 1642. Wife of Richard. She married (2) Robert Parker. She was born about 1600 (Pope).
BULGAR, RICHARD *Boston*	Probably from London or Southwark. Mason. He came as assumed 1630, having married

Bulgar, ——	married sister of Capt. John Underhill. Also removed to Dover 1638 with Capt. Underhill. Freeman 18 May 1631 (M.C.R., I, 366). Wife of Richard (Winthrop MSS.). She was 'sister' of Capt. John Underhill.
BURNELL (BUNNELL), WILLIAM *Boston*	Origin undetermined. Juryman 1630. Died 1660/1 (M.C.R., I, 77).
BURR, JEHU *Roxbury*	Origin undetermined. Freeman 18 May 1631 (M.C.R., I, 80). Carpenter. Removed with Pynchon to Springfield, and Fairfield, Conn. Probably died before 1654.
Burr, ——	Wife of Jehu (Eliot).
Burr, Jehu	Son of Jehu Senior, born 1625.
BURROUGHS, ROBERT	On the *Arbella* 1630 (Stiles Hist. of Wethersfield, 168).
CABLE, JOHN *Dorchester*	Probably from Essex. Brother-in-law of Jehu Burr. Removed to Springfield and Fairfield, Conn. First mentioned in 1631 (M.C.R., I, 85).
CAKEBREAD, THOMAS	From Hatfield Broadoak, co. Essex (Banks MSS.). Freeman 14 May 1634 (M.C.R., I, 368); Ensign 1638; removed to Dedham and died 1643. Related to Thomas Reade (q.v.), and to the second wife of John Winthrop, Jr.
Cakebread, Sarah	Wife of Thomas; she married (2) Philemon Whale.
CHADWICK, CHARLES *Watertown*	Freeman 18 May 1631 (M.C.R., I, 366). Probably from Essex. Born 1596; died 10 April 1682, aged 86.
Chadwick, Elizabeth	Wife of Charles.
CHAMBERS, ANNE or ANNIE	Mentioned in Bluette's letter from Groton 1633. Boston church 1631, No. 140.
CHASE, WILLIAM *Roxbury*	From co. Essex. Member First Church Roxbury. Applied freeman 19 Oct. 1630; (M.C.R., I, 80).

(M.C.R., I, 80). Freeman 19 May 1634 (*ibid.*, I, 369).

CHAUNER, MARGERY
Boston

Member church 1630, No. 116.

CHEESEBROUGH, WILLIAM
Boston

From Boston, co. Lincoln. Blacksmith. Born 1594. Juryman 9 Nov. 1630 (M.C.R., I, 78). Freeman 18 May 1631 (*ibid.*, I, 366). Removed to Braintree and Rehoboth.

Cheesebrough, Ann (Stevenson)　Wife of William. Born 1596. Admitted church 1630, No. 45.

Cheesebrough, Sarah　Daughter of William. Admitted church 1630, No. 78.

Cheesebrough, Peter　Son of William.

Cheesebrough, Samuel　Son of William.

Cheesebrough, Nathaniel　Son of William.

CHILD, EPHRAIM
Watertown

From Bury St. Edmunds, Suffolk, or vicinity. Applied freeman 19 Oct. 1630 (M.C.R., I, 79). Freeman 18 May 1631 (*ibid.*, I, 366). Died 13 (12) 1662/3 aged 70 (b. 1592). Bluette of Groton calls him 'my ancient acquaintance' in letter 1633.

Child, Elizabeth　Wife of Ephraim (Pope).

CHURCH, RICHARD
Boston

Perhaps from Polstead, Suffolk. Carpenter. Deposed aged 48 in 1657 (b. 1609). Removed to Weymouth, Plymouth and Charlestown. Applied freeman 19 Oct. 1630 (M.C.R., I, 80). Died 1668. He came over as a servant of 'Mr. (Richard) Webb' (Drake, Boston, 132).

CLARKE, JOHN
Boston

From Groton, Suffolk, or vicinity. Perhaps Mr. John of Braintree 1637. Mentioned in letter of Bluette of Groton 1633 as 'my scholar.' Freeman 6 Nov. 1632 (M.C.R., I, 368). Member church, 1630, No. 138.

CLARKE, WILLIAM
Watertown

Citizen and skinner of London. Applied for freeman 19 Oct. 1630, with his brother-in-law Samuel Freeman of Watertown (q.v.). Before

	Before the Court 9 Nov. 1630 (*ibid.*, 75); Freeman 18 May 1631. His wife was Elizabeth Quick, daughter of William Quick, citizen and grocer of London. He returned to England between 1631 and 1636 and was living in London in 1640 (Lechford). He did not return to New England, as far as known (Banks MSS.).
Clarke, Elizabeth	Wife of William. Returned to England and died shortly after arrival (Banks MSS.).
CLOUGH (CLUFFE), RICHARD *Charlestown*	Probably from Suffolk. Tailor. Before court 28 Sept. 1630 (M.C.R., I, 76).
COBBETT, ——	Sent back to England March 1, 1630/1 (M.C.R., I, 82).
CODDINGTON, WILLIAM *Boston*	Gentleman. Born 4 Feb. 1598/9, son of Edward and Anne (Gifforth). From Boston, England. Removed to Newport. John Beauchamp calls him 'brother' in a letter to Wm. Paddy, 1649 (Freeman Gen., 23). (M.C.R., I, 75).
Coddington, Mary	Wife of William. Died 1630 (Dudley Letter).
COLBRON, WILLIAM *Boston*	From Brentwood, Essex. Applied freeman 19 Oct. 1630 (M.C.R., I, 80). Freeman 18 May 1631 (*ibid.*, I, 366). Member church, No. 9.
Colbron, Margery	Wife of William. Member church, No. 15.
COLBY, ANTHONY *Boston*	Perhaps from Lincolnshire, near Sempringham, the seat of the Earl of Lincoln, where the name is found. Cambridge 1635; removed to Salisbury. Member church 1630, No. 93. Freeman 14 May 1634 (M.C.R., I, 369). Died 11 Feb. 1660.
Colby, Susanna (Haddon)	(Hoyt, Old Families of Salisbury, 895) Wife of Anthony. Born about 1608. Married (2) William Whitridge. Died 8 July 1689.

COLE, JOHN

COLE, JOHN *Boston*	From Groton, Suffolk, or immediate vicinity. (Winthrop MSS.).
COLE, RICE *Charlestown* Cole, Arrold	Probably from London. Member church Boston 1630, No. 109. Freeman 1 April 1633. Died 15 (3) 1646. Wife of Rice. Will dated 20 (10) 1662: probated 26 (10) 1662. 'Brother Solomon Phipps' mentioned (Pope).
COLE, ROBERT *Roxbury*	From Navestock, Essex. 'Came with first company' (Eliot). Applied freeman 19 Oct. 1630 (M.C.R., I, 80). Perhaps removed to Providence, Rhode Island, before 1644 (Winthrop).
COLE, SAMUEL *Boston* Cole, Anne	Perhaps from Mersey, co. Essex. Applied freeman 18 Oct. 1630 (M.C.R., I, 80). Confectioner. Member First Church 1630/1, No. 42. Will 21 Dec. 1666; probated 13 Feb. 1666/7. Wife of Samuel. Member church 1630/1, No. 43.
CONVERSE, EDWARD *Charlestown* Converse, Sarah Converse, Phineas Converse, John Converse, Josiah Converse, James	Probably from Shenfield, Essex, or vicinity. Juror 1630 (M.C.R., I, 77). Freeman 18 May 1631 (*ibid.*, I, 366). Deposed 24 (1) 1661/2 aged about 72 (b. 1589). Died 10 Aug. 1663 (G. R., LIX, 176). Removed to Woburn. Wife of Edward. Member church 1630, No. 84. Son of Edward. Son of Edward. Son of Edward. Born 1619. Son of Edward. Born 1621.
COOKE, MARGARET	Church member No. 56; received Boston church 1630.
COWLISHAW, WILLIAM *Boston* Cowlishaw, Anne	From Nottingham (Banks MSS.); admitted church Oct. 1633; freeman 4 March 1633/4 (M.C.R., I, 368). No further record. Wife of William.

CRABB, JOHN

CRABB, JOHN	Applied freeman 9 Oct. 1630 (M.C.R., I, 80). Nothing further known.
CRAFTS, GRIFFIN *Roxbury*	From London or Essex. Freeman 18 May 1631 (M.C.R., I, 366). Deputy and Lieutenant. Died 1690.
Crafts, Alice	Wife of Griffin. Born 1600; died 1673 aged 73 (Pope).
Crafts, Hannah	Daughter of Griffin.
CRANWELL, JOHN *Boston*	From Woodbridge, Suffolk. Applied freeman 19 Oct. 1630; freeman 4 March 1633/4. Died 1639. Thomas Marrett was brother-in-law.
CRIBB, BENJAMIN	He was punished for a misdemeanor in March 1630/1. Possibly an error for Crabb (q.v.) (M.C.R., I, 85). Nothing further known.
CRUGOTT, JAMES	On record as a juror 26 Sept. 1630, but nothing further is known about him either of his origin or residence. Probably died or left the Colony.
DADY, WILLIAM *Charlestown*	Perhaps from Wanstead, Essex, or vicinity. A butcher. Admitted church Boston 1631/2, No. 122. Born 1605; died 10 April 1682 aged 77 (g. s.). Freeman 1 April 1632/3 (M.C.R., I, 367).
Dady, Dorothy	Wife of William (Wyman, 271).
DEEKES (DIX), EDWARD *Charlestown*	Probably from Essex where families of Deekes are found. Freeman 4 March 1634/5. Member of church 1630, No. 49. Removed to Watertown.
Deekes (Dix), Jane	Wife of Edward (Pope).
DEVEREUX, JOHN	Probably from Stoke-by-Nayland, co. Suffolk. Came as a minor, as he was born about 1614, and testified that he came to New England in 1630 (G.R.).

DIFFY, RICHARD

DIFFY, RICHARD *Watertown*	Servant to Sir Richard Saltonstall (M.C.R., I, 81). No further record.
DILLINGHAM, JOHN *Boston*	From Bitteswell, Leicester. Member church 1630, No. 71. Juryman 1631. Died 1636.
Dillingham, Sarah (Caly)	Wife of John. Will 14 July 1636; probated 2 Dec. 1636.
Dillingham, Sarah	Daughter of John.
DIXON, WILLIAM *Boston*	Probably from Suffolk. Servant to Gov. Winthrop. Cooper. Died 1666. (M.C.R., I, 105). Removed to York, Me. 1636.
DOGGETT, JOHN *Watertown*	From Suffolk, vicinity of Groton. Applied freeman 19 Oct. 1630. Freeman. Removed to Martha's Vineyard. Died 1673 (M.C.R., I, 80).
Doggett, ——	Wife of John.
Doggett, John, Jr.	Son of John.
Doggett, Thomas	Son of John.
DOWNING, JAMES	Servant of Winthrop (Winthrop MSS., W-7a 38).
DUDLEY, THOMAS *Boston*	From Northamptonshire. Son of Roger and Susanna (Thorne) Dudley of Yardley, Northamptonshire. Baptized 12 Oct. 1576. Steward to Earl of Lincoln at Sempringham. He was not made a freeman until 1636 (M.C.R., I, 372).
Dudley, Dorothy (Yorke)	Wife of Thomas. 'A gentlewoman whose extraction and estate were considerable' (Cotton Mather). Died Dec. 1643.
Dudley, Samuel	Son of Thomas.
Dudley, Anne	Daughter of Thomas.
Dudley, Patience	Daughter of Thomas.
Dudley, Sarah	Daughter of Thomas (G.R., LXXV, 236).
Dudley, Mercy	Daughter of Thomas.
Dudley, Thomas, Jr.	Son of Thomas (G.R., LXXV, 236).
DUTTON, ——	In Winthrop's list, but no further record.
	EDMUNDS, JOHN

EDMUNDS, JOHN *Boston* Edmunds, Mary	Probably from Essex. Member church 1630, No. 63. Freeman 18 May 1631 (M.C.R., I, 366). Wife of John.
EGGLESTON, BIGOD *Dorchester*	From Settrington, co. York. Baptized 20 Feb. 1586. Freeman 18 May 1631 (M.C.R., I, 80). Removed to Windsor, Conn.
ELLIS, ARTHUR	Juryman 28 Sept. 1630 (M.C.R., I, 78). No further record. Probably died or returned.
ELSTON, JOHN *Salem*	Probably one of Cradock's servants (Prince, Chronology).
FAYERWEATHER, THOMAS *Boston*	Origin undetermined. Freeman 14 May 1634 (M.C.R., I, 369). Member church No. 101. Inventory estate taken 8 (11), 1638/9.
FEAKE, ROBERT, gentleman. *Watertown*	From St. Edmunds, Lombard St., London. Son of James Feake of London, goldsmith. Applied freeman 19 Oct. 1630 (M.C.R., I, 79). Freeman 18 May 1631 (*ibid.*, I, 366). Married Mrs. Elizabeth (Fones) Winthrop, widow of Henry. Removed to Long Island. Died 1662.
FIENNES, CHARLES	Brother of Earl of Lincoln. Returned to England (G.R., LXXV, 236).
FINCH, ABRAHAM *Watertown* Finch, Abraham, Jr.	Said to have been born 1585 in Yorkshire (Mead, Hist. Greenwich). Brought three sons as below. Freeman 3 Sept. 1634; removed to Wethersfield. Called 'Old Finch'; died 1638. The name Finch is found in many parishes of Essex — a more likely origin of this family. Son of above. Said to have been killed by Indians 1637.
	Finch, Daniel

Finch, Daniel	Son of Abraham, Watertown. Freeman 18 May 1631 (M.C.R., I, 365). Removed to Wethersfield where he died 27 (11) 1673/4.
Finch, John	Son of Abraham, Watertown. Removed to Wethersfield and later to Fairfield where he died 1657 (Fairfield Land Records, A-239).
FIRMAN, JOHN *Watertown*	From Nayland, co. Suffolk (Gregory Stone Genealogy). Freeman 18 May 1631 (M.C.R., I, 366).
FIRMIN, GILES, JR.	From Nayland, co. Suffolk (Waters & Emmerton). Church member No. 145. Freeman 22 May 1639 (M.C.R., I, 376).
Firmin, Martha (Doggett)	Wife of Giles.
FITZRANDOLPH, EDWARD *Scituate*	From Sutton-in-Ashfield, Notts. Came in 1630, according to diary of his grandson Nathaniel of New Jersey. Probably an apprentice when he emigrated, and perhaps one of those freed in 1630 when provisions became scarce (Dudley Letter). Several of them went to Plymouth Colony and stayed there. Fitzrandolph married in Scituate. In 1669 he removed to New Jersey (Pope).
Fox, THOMAS *Boston*	Probably from London or vicinity. Servant to Matthew Cradock. Removed to Cambridge. Born 1608; died 1693, April 25, aged 85 (M.C.R., I, 84).
FOXWELL, RICHARD *Boston*	Tailor. Freeman 18 May 1631 (M.C.R., I, 80). Removed to Plymouth, Scituate, Barnstable. Probably from St. Bridget's, London, as he was a member of Rev. John Lathrop's church which met in a near-by parish. Freeman 18 May 1631 (M.C.R., I, 80).
Foxwell, ——	Wife of Richard.
Foxwell, John	Son of Richard.

FREEMAN, SAMUEL

FREEMAN, SAMUEL	From St. Anne, Blackfriars, London. Son of John and Priscilla (?) Freeman. Probably returned to England.
Freeman, Apphia (Quick)	Wife of Samuel. Daughter of William Quick of London. She divorced him and married (2) Gov. Thomas Prence.
Freeman, Henry	Son of Samuel.
FRENCH, THOMAS *Boston*	From Assington, co. Suffolk. Settled Ipswich and died before 5 Nov. 1639.
French, Susan (Riddlesdale)	Wife of Thomas.
French, Thomas, Jr.	Son of Thomas, born 1608. Mentioned in letter of John Bluette of Groton as 'my scholar' (L. & L.W.).
French, Alice	Daughter of Thomas. Born 1610.
French, Dorcas	Daughter of Thomas. Born 1614. Maidservant to Gov. Winthrop.
French, Susan	Daughter of Thomas. Born 1616.
French, Anne	Daughter of Thomas. Born 1618.
French, John	Son of Thomas. Born 1622.
French, Mary	Daughter of Thomas. Born 1625.
FROTHINGHAM, WILLIAM *Charlestown*	From Holderness, Yorkshire (Wyman, Charlestown Genealogies). Applied freeman 19 Oct. 1630; freeman 6 March 1631/2 (M.C.R., I, 80). Died 18 (8) 1651.
Frothingham, Anne	Wife of William. Member church Boston 1630; died 28 July 1674 aged 67 (b. 1607).
GAGE, JOHN *Boston*	Probably from Polstead, Suffolk, near Groton. Member church, No. 50. Freeman 4 March 1633/4 (M.C.R., I, 368). Removed to Ipswich 1633. Died 24 March 1672/3.
Gage, Amy	Wife of John (Pope).
GAGER, WILLIAM *Charlestown*	From Suffolk. Surgeon, employed by the Massachusetts Bay Company. Died 20 Sept. 1630 (M.C.R., I, 74).
—, —	Servant to Doctor Gager, name unknown (L. & L.W.).

GARRETT, HUGH

GARRETT, HUGH	Inhabitant of Charlestown 1630 (Ch.Ch. Rec., 3).
GARRETT, RICHARD *Boston*	Probably from Chelmsford, Essex, or vicinity. Shoemaker. Member church 1630. Applied freeman 19 Oct. 1630 (M.C.R., I, 78). Died 28 Dec. 1630 (Suff. Deeds, III, 344).
Garrett, ——	Wife of Richard (Pope).
Garrett, Hannah	Daughter of Richard. Died Dec. 1632.
Garrett, ——	Daughter of Richard (Winthrop, I, 54–6).
GIBSON, CHRISTOPHER *Dorchester*	From Wendover, co. Bucks (G.R., LXV, 65). Chandler. Applied freeman 19 Oct. 1630 (M.C.R., I, 80).
Gibson, Mary	Wife of Christopher (Pope).
GIBSON, ELIZABETH	From St. Andrew the Great, Cambridge; born about 1614. Probably came with some relative, as she was married to Capt. John Endicott shortly after arrival at Salem, by Gov. Winthrop assisted by Rev. John Wilson (Winthrop).
GLOVER, RALPH *Boston*	From London. Applied freeman 19 Oct. 1630 (M.C.R., I, 79). Admin. estate 2 July 1633.
GLOVER, JOHN *Dorchester*	From Rainhill, Lancashire, son of Thomas (Suffolk Deeds, I, 333). Tanner. Did not join church until 1638. Removed to Boston. Will proved 9 Feb. 1653.
Glover, Anne ——	Wife of John.
GOLDTHWAITE, THOMAS *Roxbury*	Cooper. Entered suit against Mr. Pelham 14 June 1631. Freeman 14 May 1634 (M.C.R., I, 368). Removed to Salem, where he died 1683, aged about 75 years (Perley, History of Salem, I, 356); name not found in usual English sources.
Goldthwaite, Elizabeth	Wife of Thomas (Pope).
	GOSNALL, HENRY

GOSNALL, HENRY *Boston*	Probably from Bury St. Edmunds, Suffolk. Member church 1630, No. 29. No further record.
Gosnall, Mary	Wife of Henry. Member church 1630.
GOSSE (GOFFE), JOHN *Watertown*	Origin undetermined. Freeman 18 May 1631. Died Feb. 1643/4 (M.C.R., I, 366).
Gosse (Goffe), Sarah	Wife of John. She married (2) Robert Nichols and removed to Southampton or Southold, L.I. (Pope).
GOULWORTH, JOHN	Punished 28 Sept. 1630 (M.C.R., I, 77). No further record.
GRIDLEY, RICHARD *Boston*	From Groton, Suffolk. Mason. Deposed 2 July 1660 aged 59 years (G.R., LXXVI, 240) (B.T.R., 1631).
Gridley, Grace	Wife of Richard (G.R., LXXVI, 240) (Pope).
Gridley, Joseph	Son of Richard (G.R., LXXVI, 240).
Gridley, Abraham	Son of Richard (G.R., LXXVI, 240).
GYVER, BRIDGET *Boston*	Member church 1630, No. 147. From Saffron Walden, co. Essex.
HADDON, GARRETT *Cambridge*	English origin not determined. Cambridge 1632, Salisbury 1640. Tailor. Member church 1630/1, No. 96. Freeman 14 May 1634 (M.C.R., I, 369). Deposed 14 (2) 1668 aged about 60 (b. 1608).
Haddon, Margaret	Wife of Garrett (Hoyt, Old Families Salisbury, 191).
HALE, ROBERT *Charlestown*	Origin undetermined. Carpenter. Removed to Malden; became minister at Beverly (G.R., XIII, 315). Died 16 (5) 1659 (Ch.Ch.Rec. 1630).
Hale, Joan	Wife of Robert. She married (2) Richard Jacob (Pope).
HALL, JOHN *Charlestown*	From Whitechapel, London. Carpenter. Freeman 14 May 1634. Died about Dec. 1639 (Ch.Ch.Rec. 1630) (Savage). Hall, Joan (Dove)

Hall, Joan (Dove)	Wife of John. From Bethnal Green, Stepney. Married 1618.
HAMMOND, PHILIPPA	Widow. She married Robert Harding. Was an adherent of Mrs. Hutchinson. Member church 1630.
HARDING, ROBERT *Boston*	Probably from Boreham, Essex. Brother of Abraham. Merchant, mariner. Juror 1630 (M.C.R., I, 78). Freeman 18 May 1631 (M.C.R., I, 366). Newport 1640.
HARRIS, THOMAS *Charlestown*	This passenger appears under an 'alias Williams' when he requested admission as freeman 19 Oct. 1630; as Thomas Williams he was made freeman 19 May 1631 (M.C.R., I, 80, 366); d. 1632/3. See WILLIAMS.
Harris, Elizabeth	Wife of Thomas; she m. (2) William Stilson, 1633 (Wyman, Charlestown Gen., 467, 902).
HARWOOD, HENRY *Boston*	Probably from Shenfield, Essex. Herdman. Applied freeman 19 Oct. 1630 (M.C.R., I, 80). Freeman 4 March 1632/3. Removed to Charlestown. Inventory estate 5 (10) 1637.
Harwood, Elizabeth	Wife of Henry. Admitted church 1632 (Pope).
HAWKE, ——	In Winthrop's list, but no further record.
HAWKINS, JOHN	Church member 1630; no further record. Died soon.
HAWTHORNE, WILLIAM *Dorchester*	From Binfield, Berks. Removed to Salem. Freeman 14 May 1634 (M.C.R., I, 368). Ancestor of the famous novelist, Nathaniel Hawthorne, and a distinguished official of the Colony. (Henry F. Waters, Essex Institute, XVII, 52). HESSELDEN, FRANCIS

HESSELDEN, FRANCIS

Church member 1630, No. 34. Died soon. No further record. Perhaps from Boston, Lincolnshire.

HOAMES, MARGARET

Church member 1630, No. 20. No further record.

HOFFE, ——

This name appears in Winthrop's list minus his Christian name. No person named Hoffe is found among the early settlers but it is probable that it refers to Mr. Atherton Hough of Boston, Lincolnshire, who came to New England in 1633 with his pastor, Rev. John Cotton. He may have been a passenger with Winthrop at this time for the purpose of viewing the country and reporting on its desirability for settlement. Winthrop calls him 'Hoffe' in his Journal.

HOPWOOD, EDWARD

Returned to England 1630 (Winthrop MSS., W.I., 81).

HORNE, JOHN

English origin undetermined. Carpenter. Freeman 18 May 1631 (M.C.R., I, 366). Deposed in 1662, aged 60.

HOSIER, SAMUEL
Watertown

From Colchester, Essex (Lechford). Planter. Freeman 18 May 1631. Died 29 July 1665 (M.C.R., I, 80).

HOWLETT, THOMAS
Boston

From co. Suffolk, England. Removed Ipswich 1633. Deposed 1658, aged 52. Church member 1630.

HUDSON, WILLIAM
Boston

Probably from Chatham, Kent. Baker. Freeman 18 May 1631 (Ch. Rec., 1630). Returned to England and became Ensign in Col. Rainsborough's regiment.

Hudson, Susan
Hudson, Francis
Hudson, William, Jr.

Wife of William (Boston Ch. Rec.) (Pope). Son of William. Born 1611 (Pope). Son of William (Pope).

HULBIRT, WILLIAM

HULBIRT, WILLIAM
Boston

Origin undetermined. Removed to Windsor, Hartford, Northampton. Freeman 2 April 1632 (M.C.R., I, 367).

HUTCHINS, RICHARD

Applied freeman 18 May 1630 (M.C.R., I, 80). No further record.

HUTCHINSON, GEORGE
Charlestown
Hutchinson, Margaret

From London. Member church 1630, No. 53. Freeman 1 April 1634 (M.C.R., I, 368). Wife of George (Pope).

HUTCHINSON, THOMAS
Charlestown

From London. Member church 1630 No. 52. Marked 'dead.'

IJONS (IRONS), MATTHIAS

Ijons (Irons), Anne

Probably from Danbury or Roxwell, co. Essex. Servant of William Colborn who came 1630. Had child baptized 5 April 1631 (Boston Ch. Rec.).
Wife of Matthias (Boston Ch. Rec.).

JAMES, EDMOND
Watertown

James, Reana

From Earl's Barton, co. Northants. Applied freeman 19 Oct. 1630 (M.C.R., I, 80). Died before 1640.
Wife of Edmond (Pope). She married (2) William Andrews (Middlesex Deeds III, 7).

JAMES, THOMAS
Salem
James, Elizabeth

From Earl's Barton, Member church 1630, No. 149.
Wife of Thomas. Member church, No. 150.

JAMES, WILLIAM
Salem
James, Elizabeth

From Earl's Barton, co. Northants. Applied freeman 19 Oct. 1630 (M.C.R., I, 80). Wife of William.

JARVIS, JOHN
Boston

Juryman 28 Sept. 1630 (M.C.R., I, 78). Died 1656.

JOHNSON, DAVY
Dorchester

Freeman 18 May 1631 (M.C.R., I, 366). Died 1636.

JOHNSON, FRANCIS
Salem

Probably from London. Merchant. Nephew of Christopher Colson, an Assistant of the Mass. Bay Company 1629 (M.C.R., IV, 429).

Johnson, Joan

(M.C.R., IV, 429). Freeman 18 May 1631 (M.C.R., I, 366). Deposed in 1672, aged 66. Wife of Francis (Pope).

JOHNSON, ISAAC
Salem

Born 1601, died Sept. 1630. Son of Abraham Johnson, Esq. of So. Luffenham, co. Rutland, but resided at Clipsham, same county. Married (lic. 5 April 1623) the Lady Arbella, daughter of Thomas, third Earl of Lincoln (M.C.R., I, 78). He was the Founder of Boston (Prince, N.E. Chronology, 249).

Johnson, Arbella

From Sempringham, Lincolnshire. Born 1601; died Aug. 1630 (M.C.R., I, 78).

JOHNSON, JOHN
Roxbury

Origin undetermined. Freeman 18 May 1631. Constable 19 Oct. 1630. Died 30 (7) 1659 (M.C.R., I, 75).

Johnson, Margaret

Wife of John. Died 9 (4) 1655 (Pope).

JOHNSON, RICHARD
Charlestown

Removed to Salem. Deposed 1663 aged 51. Freeman 17 May 1637 (M.C.R., I, 367). He was here before court in March 1631 (M.C.R., I, 84). Origin undetermined.

Johnson, Alice

Wife of Richard (Pope).

JONES, BETHIA
Boston

Member church 1630 (Boston Ch. Rec.). Removed to Salem (Pope).

JONES, EDWARD
Charlestown

From Chester. Mercer. (Harl. MSS., 1972 fo. 44d) Freeman 18 May 1631 (M.C.R., I, 366). He sold his house and lands in 1644. No further record.

KIDBY, LEWIS
Boston

The identity of this passenger is not established, but he was probably a neighbor of Governor Winthrop in Groton. In a letter to his wife he mentions the death of 'one of L. Kidbys sons.' It is therefore probable that one of the name living later in Boston was one who survived (L. & L.W., II).

Kidby, ——
Kidby, ——

Wife of Lewis.
Son of above. Died 1630.

Kidby, Edward

Kidby, Edward	A sawyer, living in Boston and later in Roxbury, with a family.
KINGSBURY, HENRY *Boston*	Came in the *Talbot* from Groton, Suffolk. First Church member No. 25. Died soon after arrival (Winthrop).
Kingsbury, Margaret	Wife of Henry. First Church member, No. 26.
Kingsbury, Henry, Jr.	Son of Henry. Born 1615; died 1 Oct. 1687. Ipswich, Rowley, Haverhill (Pope).
KINGSBURY, THOMAS	In Gov. Winthrop's list. No further record. Died or returned.
KNAPP, NICHOLAS *Watertown*	Probably from Bures St. Mary, Suffolk. Sold his land, etc., 6 (3) 1646 (Frost Gen. p. 372). Sold medicine for the scurvy (M.C.R., I, 83).
Knapp, Elinor	Wife of Nicholas (B.T.R.).
KNAPP, WILLIAM *Watertown*	Probably from Bures St. Mary, co. Suffolk. Born about 1579; died 30 Aug. 1659. Mentioned 3 Nov. 1630 in Colonial Records (M.C.R., I, 82).
Knapp, ——	Wife of William.
Knapp, John	Son of William (Pope).
Knapp, Anne	Daughter of William (Pope).
Knapp, Judith	Daughter of William (Pope).
Knapp, Mary	Daughter of William (Pope).
Knapp, James	Son of William (Pope).
Knapp, John	Son of William (Pope).
Knapp, William, Jr.	Son of William (Pope).
KNOWER, GEORGE *Charlestown*	Probably from London. Born 1607; died 13 Feb. 1674 aged 67 (Lechford, 203).
KNOWER, THOMAS *Charlestown*	From London. Clothier (Pope).
LAMB, EDWARD *Watertown*	Origin not determined. Among first settlers of Watertown (Bond). Died about 1650 and widow Margaret married (2) Samuel Allen (Pope).

LAMB, THOMAS

LAMB, THOMAS *Roxbury*	Perhaps from Stowe Langtoft, co. Suffolk. Freeman 18 May 1631 (M.C.R., I, 366). Died 3 April 1646.
Lamb, Elizabeth	Wife of Thomas. Buried 28 Nov. 1639 (Pope).
Lamb, Thomas, Jr.	Son of Thomas (Eliot).
Lamb, John	Son of Thomas (Eliot).
Lamb, Samuel	Son of Thomas (Eliot).
LAMB, ROGER	Origin not determined. Freeman 18 May 1631 (M.C.R., I, 366). No residence known and no further record.
LAWSON, HENRY	Probably from London. Mentioned 14 June 1631 (M.C.R., I, 88). No further record.
LEARNED, WILLIAM *Charlestown*	Probably from Bermondsey, Surrey. Freeman 14 May 1634 (M.C.R., I, 368). Died 1 March 1645 (Pope).
Learned, Judith	Wife of William. Admitted church 6 (10) 1632 (Ch.Ch.Rec.).
LEATHERLAND, WILLIAM *Boston*	Origin undetermined, but probably London, as he was servant of Owen Rowe, a silk merchant of All Hallows, Honey Lane, London, one of the members of the Massachusetts Bay Company. Leatherland was a carpenter, born 1608. Admitted church 24 Nov. 1633; freeman 4 March 1634/5 (M.C.R., I, 370).
LEGGE, JOHN *Lynn*	Probably from London. In the service of Mr. John Humphrey 3 May 1631 (M.C.R., I, 86). Deposed 1657, aged 45 (b. 1612). Will proved 2 (5) 1674.
LOCKWOOD, EDMOND *Cambridge*	Son of Edmond. From Combs, Suffolk. Baptized 9 Feb. 1594. Winthrop writes about money to be paid to Downing for Lockwood: 'let Mr. Peirce be payd his bill of provisions for him and bring the rest with

Lockwood, Elizabeth	with you' (Winthrop MSS., W. 7a 45). He died before 1635, leaving widow Ruth. Wife of Edmond (Pope). Died soon.
Lockwood, ——	Child of Edmond.
LOCKWOOD, ROBERT	Son of Edmond of Combs, Suffolk. Baptized 18 Jan. 1600. Probably brother of Edmond (Banks MSS.). He may be the 'Sergeant' following the name of Lockwood in Winthrop's list to distinguish the two brothers.
LYNTON, RICHARD *Watertown*	Probably from St. Botolph, Aldgate, London. Juror 28 Sept. 1630 (M.C.R., I, 78). Died 30 (11) 1665.
Lynton, ——	Wife of Richard (Pope).
Lynton, Anna	Daughter of Richard (Pope).
Lynton, Lydia	Daughter of Richard (Pope).
LYNN, HENRY	Origin undetermined. In court 28 Sept. 1630. Whipped and banished Sept. 1631 (M.C.R., I, 77, 91). Removed to Agamenticus (York), Maine, and died about 1644 in Virginia.
Lynn, Sarah	Wife of Henry (Pope).
MASTERS, JOHN *Watertown*	Probably from Suffolk. Freeman 18 May 1631 (M.C.R., I, 366). Removed to Cambridge. Died 21 Dec. 1639.
Masters, Jane	Wife of John.
Masters, Sarah	Daughter of John (Pope).
Masters, Lydia	Daughter of John (Pope).
Masters, Elizabeth	Daughter of John (Pope).
Masters, Nathaniel	Son of John (Pope).
Masters, Abraham	Son of John (Pope).
MATSON, THOMAS	From London. Admitted church 1630, No. 85. Will 9 June 1676; probated 26 April 1677. Freeman 4 March 1633/4 (M.C.R., I, 368).
Matson, Amy (or Ann)	Wife of Thomas. She was sister-in-law of Mrs. Chambers, widow of Thomas, citizen and cloth-worker of St. Mary Abchurch, London (Pope).

MAYHEW, THOMAS

MAYHEW, THOMAS *Watertown*	From Southampton probably, but born in 1592 at Tisbury, co. Wilts. Died at Martha's Vineyard (Banks, Hist. of Martha's Vineyard).
Mayhew,	Wife of Thomas, Sr. She died soon after arrival.
Mayhew, Thomas, Jr.	Son of Thomas. The famous Indian missionary. Lost at sea 1657 (Banks, Hist. Martha's Vineyard).
MILLER, ——	In Winthrop's list, but no further record.
MILLETT, RICHARD	Perhaps from London or Southwark. Applied for freeman 18 Oct. 1630 (M.C.R., I, 80); freeman 11 June 1633 (M.C.R., I, 368). No further record.
MILLS, JOHN *Boston*	Perhaps from Lavenham, co. Suffolk. Said he was descended from a line of ministers 'unto the third if not the fourth generations' (will). Member church No. 33. Applied freeman 19 Oct. 1630 (M.C.R., I, 80); freeman March 1631/2 (*ibid.*, I, 367). Died 5 July 1678.
Mills, Susan	Wife of John. Member church No. 34. Died 10 (10) 1675, aged 80 years (Pope).
Mills, Joy	Daughter of John (Pope).
Mills, Mary	Daughter of John. Married James Hawkins (Pope).
Mills, John, Jr.	Son of John (Pope).
Mills, Susanna	Daughter of John. Married William Dawes (Pope).
Mills, Recompense	Daughter of John (Pope).
MOREY, ROGER *Salem*	This name appears as Moorey and Mowry. Origin undetermined. Freeman 18 May 1631 (M.C.R., I, 366). He removed to Rhode Island.
MORLEY, RALPH *Charlestown*	From London. Died Sept. 1630 (Pope).
Morley, Catherine	Widow of Ralph (Pope) (Wyman, 685).

MORRIS, RICHARD

MORRIS, RICHARD *Boston*	Probably from London. Held military rank and wrote a Latin epistle to Capt. John Underhill (Lechford). Removed to Dover 1639. Member First Church 1630 (M.C.R., I, 81). Probably removed to Portsmouth, R.I. about 1641. No further record in Massachusetts after 1654.
Morris, Lenora	Wife of Richard. Member church 1630 (Pope). She was called 'agged and weak' in 1647 (Documentary Hist., R.I., II, 180).
MORRIS, THOMAS *Boston*	Probably from Nottingham; died early (Savage).
Morris, Sarah	Wife of Thomas, daughter of William and Anne Cowlishaw (q.v.).
MORTON, MARY	She may have come from Colchester and was a servant of Mrs. Downing in 1629 (L. & L.W., 291). Probably the 'Mary M' one of the servants of Winthrop mentioned in letter to his wife 2 March 1629/30 (*ibid.*). Church member No. 86.
MOULTON, THOMAS *Charlestown*	Origin undetermined. Fisherman and Master of Ralph Glover's boat 3 Nov. 1630 (M.C.R., I, 82). Deposed 4 (4) 1639, aged 30 (b. 1609).
Moulton, Jane	Wife of Thomas. Deposed 1654, aged 45 (b. 1609).
MOUSALL, RALPH *Charlestown*	Probably from London. Recorded as freeman 18 May 1631 as 'Rafe Mushell' (M.C.R., I, 366). Deposed 1663, aged 67 (b. 1596). Died 27 March 1665.
Mousall, Alice	Wife of Ralph (Pope).
MUNT, THOMAS *Boston*	Probably from Colchester, Essex, or vicinity. Mason; apprentice to Richard Garrett (Winthrop) (Suffolk Deeds III). He died in 1664.
Munt, Dorothy	Wife of Thomas. She died 28 (12) 1639.

NASH, GREGORY

NASH, GREGORY *Charlestown*	Died 1630 (Ch.Ch.Rec.).
Nash, ——	Wife of Gregory. Died 1630 (Ch.Ch.Rec.).
NEEDHAM, ANN	Member church 1630, No. 100. Nothing further is known of her or of her relationship to others of the name living in the Colony.
NICOLLS, ——	In Gov. Winthrop's list. No further record. Died or returned.
NOWELL, INCREASE *Charlestown*	From Trinity the Less, Minories, London. Although an Assistant he did not apply for freeman with the rest and was not elected until 25 May 1636 (M.C.R., I, 372). Member of First Church, No. 5. Died 1 Nov. 1655.
Nowell, Parnell (Gray) Parker	Wife of Increase. Member of First Church, No. 13. She died 25 March 1687 aged 84. She was of a Harwich, Essex, family.
ODLIN, JOHN	See AUDLEY.
PAGE, JOHN *Watertown*	From Dedham, Essex (Wheeler, Hist. of Stonington, 502). Applied for freeman 19 Oct. 1630 (M.C.R., I, 79). Freeman 18 May 1631 (*ibid.*, I, 366). Died 18 Dec. 1676 aged about 90 (b. 1586).
Page, Phebe (Paine)	Wife of John. Died 25 Sept. 1677, aged about 87 (Hammond Gen., I, 59).
Page, John	Son of John. Freeman 8 Oct. 1640 (M.C.R., I, 378).
Page, Daniel	Son of John (Pope).
PAINTER, THOMAS	Juryman 28 Sept. 1630 (M.C.R., I, 78). Freeman 12 Oct. 1640 (*ibid.*, I, 378). He became an Anabaptist (Winthrop).
Painter, Katherine	Wife of Thomas. She died 1641 (Pope).
PALMER, ABRAHAM *Charlestown*	From Canterbury, Kent (Banks MSS). Merchant. Died at Barbados about 1653. Palmer, Grace

Palmer, Grace	Wife of Abraham. Died Dec. 1660 (Pope).
PALSFORD, EDWARD	His passage money of £5 was paid, but nothing more is known of him. Either died or returned (L. & L.W., 22 March 1629/30).
PALSGRAVE, RICHARD *Charlestown*	Descent claimed from a Norfolk family. Probably from London. Applied freeman 19 Oct. 1630 (M.C.R., I, 80); freeman 18 May 1631 (*ibid.*, I, 366). Member of First Church, No. 105. Physician. Died between June and October 1651.
Palsgrave, Anne	Wife of Richard. Member of First Church, No. 106. She returned to Stepney, England, before 1656 but came back to New England where she died 17 (11) 1669, aged 75 (Pope).
Palsgrave, John	Son of Richard (Pope).
Palsgrave, Anna	Daughter of Richard (Pope).
Palsgrave, Mary	Daughter of Richard (Pope).
Palsgrave, Sarah	Daughter of Richard (Pope).
PARKE, ROBERT	Probably from Bures, co. Suffolk, or vicinity. Born about 1585. Came in *Arbella* (Stiles, Hist. of Wethersfield). He married (2) Mrs. Alice Thompson, widow of John of Preston, co. Northants. May be related to Edward Parke who called Winthrop 'cousin' (see G.R., XL, 38; XLIX, 455. Also Parke Gen.).
Parke, Martha (Chaplin)	Wife of Robert (Hist. of Wethersfield).
Parke, Thomas	Son of Robert. He married Dorothy Thompson, daughter of his father's second wife, and lived in Stonington and New London.
Parke, ——	Child of Robert (Hist. Wethersfield).
Parke, ——	Child of Robert (Hist. Wethersfield).
Parke, ——	Child of Robert (Hist. Wethersfield).
PARKER, ROBERT *Boston*	Perhaps from Manchester, co. Lancaster. Savage (III, 355) thinks from Woolpit, Suffolk. Deposed 1670 aged 66. Servant to Wm. Aspinwall. Admitted church 9 (1) 1634.

1634. Freeman 4 March 1634/5 (M.C.R., I, 370). Removed to Cambridge. Married Judith, widow Richard Bugby, who died 1682 aged 80. He died 21 March 1685, aged about 82 years.

PATRICK, CAPTAIN DANIEL
Watertown

Freeman 18 May 1631 (M.C.R., I, 366). One of the military officers employed by the Company. Formerly served in Holland. Removed to Connecticut where he was killed about March 1643.

Patrick, ——

Wife of Daniel. She was a Dutch woman (Winthrop).

PELHAM, WILLIAM
Boston

Applied freeman 19 Oct. 1630 (M.C.R., I, 79). No record of election as freeman. Removed to Sudbury. Captain 1645.

PEMBERTON, JAMES
Charlestown

Origin undetermined but probably from Essex. Freeman 19 Oct. 1630 (M.C.R., I, 80). He died 5 Feb. 1661/2.

Pemberton, Alice

Wife of James.

PEMBERTON, JOHN

Brother of James. Member church 1632 (Pope). Freeman 1 April 1634 (M.C.R., I, 368). Returned to England and died in 1654 at Lawford, co. Essex (G.R., XXXIX, 61).

Pemberton, Elizabeth

Wife of John (Pope).

PENN, JAMES
Boston

Probably from London. Appointed a beadle to attend the Governor 23 Aug. 1630 (M.C.R., I, 74). Applied freeman 19 Oct. 1630 (*ibid.*, I, 79). Will 29 (7) 1671; probated 23 (8) 1671. Member church 1630, No. 31.

Penn, Katherine

Wife of James. Member church, No. 32. Will 25 Oct. 1679 (Suffolk Probate).

PENN, WILLIAM
Charlestown

From Birmingham, co. Warwick (Mass. Archives, VIII, 92). Removed to Braintree. Shoemaker (Ch.Ch.Rec., 3).

PENNIMAN, JAMES

PENNIMAN, JAMES *Boston*	From Widford, co. Essex. Member church, No. 117. Freeman 6 March 1631/2 (M.C.R., I, 367). Removed to Braintree. He died 26 (10) 1664.
Penniman, Lydia	Wife of James. Sister of John Eliot. She married (2) Thomas Wight. Member church, No. 118.
PERRY, ISAAC	Origin not determined. Member church 1630, No. 119. Freeman 6 March 1631/2 (M.C.R., I, 367). No further record.
PETERS (PETTIT), ANNE	'Received from Salem.' Member church 1630, No. 104. From Saffron Walden.
PHILLIPS, REV. GEORGE *Watertown*	A native of Raynham, co. Norfolk, but at time of emigration was preaching at Boxford, Suffolk. Died 1 July 1644 (M.C.R., I, 73).
Phillips, ——	Wife of Rev. George. She was daughter of Richard Sergeant. Died 1630 (Dudley Letter).
Phillips, Samuel	Son of Rev. George (Bond).
Phillips, Abigail	Daughter of Rev. George (Bond).
Phillips, Elizabeth	Daughter of Rev. George (Bond).
PHILLIPS, JOHN *Dorchester*	Applied freeman 19 Oct. 1630 (M.C.R., I, 80). Freeman 7 Aug. 1632 (*ibid.*, I, 367). Removed to Boston. Died 1683.
Phillips, Joan	Wife of John. Died 1675, aged 80 (gravestone).
PHILLIPS, JOHN *Boston*	Another of the name; came over as a servant and was released from apprenticeship the first year; removed to Plymouth, where his Master sold his time to another (?) (Drake, History of Boston, 132); probably identical with John Phillips, later of Duxbury, where he lived and died in 1691, aged 89 years (Pope).
PICKERING, JOHN *Cambridge*	Probably from Suffolk, Sudbury district. Before court Sept. 1630 (M.C.R., I, 77). Pickering, Esther

Pickering, Esther	Wife of John.
Pickering, George	Son of John.
Pickering, John, Jr.	Son of John.
Pickering, Joan	Daughter of John.

PICKWORTH, JOHN — Origin unknown; came as a servant and was released during the famine period; removed to Plymouth and married (G.R., II, 243).

PIERCE, JOHN *Dorchester*	Cooper. Freeman 18 May, 1631 (M.C.R., I, 366). He died 1661 (Pope).
Pierce, Parnell	Wife of John. Died Oct. 1639 (Pope).
Pierce, Experience	Daughter of John (Pope).
Pierce, Mercy	Daughter of John (Pope).
Pierce, Samuel	Son of John (Pope).

PLAISTOW, JOSIAH, gentleman. *Boston* — From Ramsden Crays, Essex. Sent back to England 1 March 1630/1 (M.C.R., I, 82).

POLLARD, MRS. ANNE — See Appendix E.

POND, JOHN *Boston* — From Groton, Suffolk (Winthrop MSS.). Returned to England.

POND, ROBERT *Dorchester* — From Groton, Suffolk (Winthrop MSS.). Carpenter. Died 1637.

Pond, Mary — Wife of Robert. She married (2) John Blackman.

PORTER, JOHN *Roxbury* — Perhaps from Bromfield, Essex. (Banks MSS.). Freeman 5 November 1633 (M.C.R. I, 368). Removed to Boston and allied himself with the supporters of Mrs. Hutchinson and Wheelwright and soon removed to Rhode Island (1638) settling at Newport. Assistant 1641 was of Portsmouth 1655 and Wickford 1674 (Hazard, II, 612).

Porter, Margaret	Wife of John.
Porter, ——	Child of John.
Porter, ——	Child of John.
Porter, ——	Child of John.
Porter, ——	Child of John.

PRATT, DR. ABRAHAM

PRATT, DR. ABRAHAM *Roxbury*	Came from London. Had served as surgeon in Holland with English Army. Juror 1630 (M.C.R., I, 77). Applied freeman 19 Oct. 1630 (M.C.R., I, 80). He and his wife were lost at sea off the coast of Spain 1644.
Pratt, Jane	Wife of Abraham (Pope).

PYNCHON, WILLIAM, gentleman. From Writtle, co. Essex. Founder of
Dorchester Springfield which he named for a parish adjoining his ancestral home. Returned to England in 1662 and died there (M.C.R., I, 73). Although an Assistant he was not in sympathy with the Puritan rule and a book he had written on a theological subject was burned in the Public Square in 1651 at Boston.

Pynchon, Agnes	Wife of William. Died 1630 (Dudley Letter).
Pynchon, John	Son of William.
Pynchon, Anne	Daughter of William (G.R., LXXV, 236).
Pynchon, Mary	Daughter of William (G.R. LXXV, 236).
Pynchon, Margaret	Daughter of William (G.R. LXXV, 236).
RAINSFORD, EDWARD	Cooper, merchant. Freeman 17 April 1637 (M.C.R., I, 373). Member church 1630, No. 62. Deposed 29 (10) 1671, aged about 60 years. The English historian of this family has not identified him.
Rainsford, ——	Wife of Edward. Died June 1632 (Pope).
RATCLIFFE, PHILIP *Salem*	Probably from London, a servant of Cradock. For 'malicious speeches' against government convicted 14 June, 1631; to have ears cut off (M.C.R., I, 88). Roger Clapp said he saw the execution of this barbarous sentence (Memoirs).
RAWLINS, THOMAS *Roxbury*	Probably from Essex (vicinity of Nazing) where the name is very common. Carpenter. Applied freeman 19 Oct. 1630; freeman 18 May 1631 (M.C.R., I, 80, 366). Died 15 March 1660.
Rawlins, Mary	Wife of Thomas. Died 1639 (Eliot). Rawlins, Thomas, Jr.

Rawlins, Thomas, Jr.	Son of Thomas (Pope).
Rawlins, Nathaniel	Son of Thomas (Pope).
Rawlins, John	Son of Thomas (Pope).
Rawlins, Joan	Daughter of Thomas (Pope).
Rawlins, Mary	Daughter of Thomas (Pope).
READE, THOMAS *Salem*	From Wickford, Essex. Juror 28 Sept. 1630 (M.C.R., I, 78). Freeman 1 April 1634 (*ibid.*, I, 368). He returned to England.
Reade, Priscilla	Wife of Thomas. She was daughter of John Banks of Maidstone, Kent.
READING, JOSEPH *Boston*	Origin undetermined. Member church, No. 95. Removed to Cambridge 1633 and later to Ipswich where he died 1681.
READING, MILES	Origin undetermined. Cooper. Freeman 14 May 1634 (M.C.R., I, 368). Member church, No. 82. Died 1671.
REEDER, ——	In Gov. Winthrop's list. No further record. Died or returned.
REVELL, JOHN	From London. Fishmonger. Assistant. Returned in the *Lyon* 1630 (Winthrop); (Dudley Letter).
REYNOLDS, ROBERT *Boston*	Probably from Boxford, co. Suffolk. Born about 1580 (Gen. of Robert Reynolds, 7). Cordwainer. First mentioned 1632. Admitted church 1634. Freeman 3 Sept. 1634 (M.C.R., I, 369).
Reynolds, Mary	Wife of Robert.
Reynolds, Nathaniel	Son of Robert.
Reynolds, Ruth	Daughter of Robert.
Reynolds, Tabitha	Daughter of Robert.
Reynolds, Sarah	Daughter of Robert.
RICHARDSON, EZEKIEL *Charlestown*	From Westmill, co. Herts. Planter. Freeman 18 May 1631 (M.C.R., I, 366). Died 21 Oct. 1647 (Ch.Ch.Rec., 3).
Richardson, Susanna	Wife of Ezekiel. She married (2) Henry Brookes (Pope).

ROYSE (RYSE), ROBERT

ROYSE (RYSE), ROBERT *Boston*	Possibly from Exning, Suffolk. No. 137 in church list of 1630. Freeman 1 April 1634 (M.C.R., I, 368).
Royse (Ryse), Elizabeth	Wife of Robert.
RUGGLES, JOHN *Boston*	Probably from Glemsford, Suffolk. Church member No. 129. Freeman July 1632 (M.C.R., I, 367).
Ruggles, Frances	Wife of John. Church member No. 37 in 1630.
Ruggles, ——	Daughter of John. Died 1631 (Prince, II, 17, 69).
RUGGLES, JEFFREY	From Sudbury, Suffolk. 'Died soon' (Ch.Ch.Rec.).
Ruggles, Margaret	Wife of Jeffrey. Church member No. 47 (Ch.Ch.Rec.) 1630.
SALES, JOHN	From Lavenham, co. Suffolk. Member church 1630, No. 21 (Ch.Ch.Rec., 3).
Sales, ——	Wife of John.
Sales, Phebe	Daughter of John (Pope).
SALTONSTALL, SIR RICHARD *Watertown*	Of the family of Saltonstall of Yorkshire, but came from London. Freeman 18 May, 1631 (M.C.R., I, 73). He returned to England.
Saltonstall, Richard, Jr.	Son of Sir Richard (Winthrop).
Saltonstall, Samuel	Son of Sir Richard (Winthrop).
Saltonstall, Robert	Son of Sir Richard (Winthrop).
Saltonstall, Rosamond	Daughter of Sir Richard (Winthrop).
Saltonstall, Grace	Daughter of Sir Richard (Winthrop).
SAMPSON, ROBERT	From Kersey, Suffolk. He either died or returned, probably the former (L. & L.W., I, 68).
SANFORD, JOHN *Boston*	From Essex county, perhaps High Ongar. Merchant. Church member No. 115. Freeman April 1632 (M.C.R., I, 367). Removed to Rhode Island.
SAXTON, REV. GILES *Charlestown*	From Yorkshire (Magnalia, III, 214, and Lechford P. D.). Juror Sept. 1630 (M.C.R., I, 77).

I, 77). Freeman 18 May 1631 (*ibid.*, I, 366). Probably returned to England.

SCOTT, ROBERT
Boston

Probably from London (servant of John Sanford); admitted church 15 Dec. 1633; haberdasher. Freeman 10 Sept. 1636 (M.C.R., I, 372); died 1653 (G.L.).

SEAMAN, JOHN
Watertown

Probably from Suffolk, but Genealogy states born in Essex (Seaman Gen., 13).

SEELY, ROBERT
Watertown

Origin undetermined. Applied freeman 19 Oct. 1630 (M.C.R., I, 80). Freeman 18 May 1631 (M.C.R., I, 366). Removed to Wethersfield, New Haven, Saybrook, and Stratford, Conn., and New York in succession, dying in 1668 in the latter place (Savage).

SERGEANT, ——

This name appears in Winthrop's list, but no further record has been found. No person of this name is known to have come to New England as early as 1630, and it is possible that Winthrop meant to designate 'Sergeant' Robert Lockwood by his title as the name appears next to the one believed to refer to Edmond Lockwood (see under Lockwood).

SHARP, ROBERT
Boston

Probably from Roxwell, Essex. Lived near the Neck (G.L.). No further record; probably died early or returned to England.

SHARPE, THOMAS
Boston

From London. Leather-seller. Member of church, No. 6. His house burned 16 March 1630/1 (Winthrop). Returned to England.
Sharpe, —— Wife of Thomas.
Sharpe, —— Daughter of Thomas. Died 3 Jan. 1630/1.
Sharpe, Thomas Son of Thomas.

SHUT, ——

Sent back to England 1 March 1630/1 (M.C.R., I, 82).

SIMPSON, ——

SIMPSON, ——	In Winthrop's list, but nothing further known of him.
SMEAD, ——	From Coggeshall, Essex. No further record. Probably died soon.
Smead, Judith	Wife of —— Smead. Sister of Israel Stoughton (Savage).
Smead, William	Son of Mrs. Judith (Savage).
SMITH, ——	From Buxhall, Suffolk. 'Died soon' (L. & L.W.).
Smith, ——	Wife of preceding (L. & L.W.).
Smith, ——	Child of preceding. 'Died soon' (*ibid.*).
Smith, ——	Child of preceding. 'Died soon' (*ibid.*).
SMYTH, FRANCIS *Roxbury*	Perhaps from Dunmow, co. Essex. Cardmaker. Juror 1630 (M.C.R., I, 77). Freeman 18 May 1631 (*ibid.*, I, 366).
Smyth, ——	Wife of Francis. She was buried 15 March 1639 (Pope).
SQUIRE, THOMAS *Charlestown*	Probably from London. Freeman 14 May 1634 (M.C.R., I, 368). Church member 1630, No. 83.
STEARNS, ISAAC *Watertown*	From Stoke Nayland, Suffolk. Tailor. Freeman 18 May 1631 (M.C.R., I, 366). Died 19 June 1671 (M.C.R., I, 86).
Stearns, Mary (Barker)	Wife of Isaac. Daughter of John Barker of Stoke Nayland (Bond).
Sterns, John	Son of Isaac (Bond).
Stearns, Abigail	Daughter of Isaac (Bond).
Stearns, Elizabeth	Daughter of Isaac (Bond).
Stearns, Hannah	Daughter of Isaac (Bond).
Stearns, Mary	Daughter of Isaac (Bond).
STILEMAN, ELIAS *Salem*	From St. Andrew Undershaft, London, where he married Judith Adams 28 Aug. 1614. Freeman 3 July 1632 (M.C.R., I, 367).
Stileman, Judith (Adams)	Wife of Elias.
Stileman, Elias, Jr.	Son of above, 1616.
STOUGHTON, ISRAEL *Dorchester*	From Coggeshall, Essex. Was opposed to the rule of Winthrop and disfranchised for writing

Stoughton, Elizabeth

writing an heretical book. Returned to England and fought under Cromwell in the Civil War, with the rank of Lieutenant Colonel in Rainsborough's regiment (Savage). He died 1644 at Lincoln.
Wife of Israel.

STOUGHTON, THOMAS
Dorchester

From Coggeshall, Essex. Brother of Israel. Constable 28 Sept. 1630. Applied freeman 19 Oct. 1630 (M.C.R., I, 80); freeman 18 May 1631 (*ibid.*, 366). Married to Mrs. Margaret Huntington, widow of Simon, in 1635. He removed to Windsor, Conn. where he died in 1642.

Stoughton, ——

Wife of Thomas (Savage).

SUMNER, WILLIAM
(*Dorchester*

Born in Bicester, co. Oxford. Baptized 27 Jan. 1604/5. Son of Roger and Joan (Franklin). Died 9 Dec. 1688. (Genealogy).

Sumner, Mary (West)

Wife of William. Married 22 Oct. 1625. Died 7 June 1676 (Pope).

Sumner, William, Jr.

Son of William (Pope).

SWADDON, PHILIP
Watertown

One of his name was living in Hilmarton, Wiltshire, 1620 (P.C.C., 23, Soame). Servant to Robert Seely, but purchased his freedom 1631 and removed to Kittery, Maine. He was born 1600 and was living in 1673.

SWANSON, ANNA

Member First Church, No. 141.

TALMADGE, WILLIAM
Boston

From Newton Stacey, co. Hants. Carpenter. Freeman 14 May 1634 (M.C.R., I, 369). Member First Church, No. 59. Removed to Lynn.

Talmadge, ——

Wife of William. Died early (Pope).

TAYLOR, GREGORY
Watertown

Member First Church 1630, No. 76. Freeman 14 May 1634 (M.C.R., I, 369). Removed to Stamford, Conn. where he died 1657.

Taylor, Achsah

Wife of Gregory (Bond).

TAYLOR, JOHN

TAYLOR, JOHN *Boston*	From Haverhill, Suffolk (L. & L.W.). Applied freeman 19 Oct. 1630; freeman 18 May 1631 (M.C.R., I, 80, 366). Removed to Lynn.
Taylor, ——	Wife of John. Died soon after arrival (L. & L.W.).
Taylor, ——	Child of John. Died soon. (L. & L.W.).
TIMEWELL, WILLIAM	Returned to England in 1630 (Winthrop MSS.).
TOMLINS, EDWARD *Lynn*	From London. Freeman 18 May 1631 (M.C.R., I, 366). Was deputy and Clerk of the Writs (Savage).
TURNER, NATHANIEL *Saugus*	Probably from London. Applied freeman 19 Oct. 1630 (M.C.R., I, 79); freeman 3 July 1632 (M.C.R., I, 367). Removed to New Haven. Captain, deputy.
TURNER, ROBERT	Probably from Southwark, Surrey, the origin of his master Edward Bendall; admitted church 8 Sept. 1633; freeman 4 March 1633/4 (M.C.R., I, 368); innholder; died 1664.
TYNDAL, ARTHUR *Boston*	Son of Sir John. From Great Maplestead, Essex (L. & L.W., I, 17). Brother-in-law to Gov. Winthrop. Returned in *Lyon* 1631 (*ibid.*, II, 36).
UNDERHILL, JOHN *Boston*	Came directly from Holland where he had been a captain in the military service, but probably from Kenilworth, co. Warwick. Freeman 18 May 1634 (M.C.R., I, 75).
Underhill, Helen	Wife of Capt. John (Winthrop). She was a Dutch woman, living in Gornichem, whom he married in 1628.
VASSALL, WILLIAM	Assistant. From Prittlewell, Essex. Returned to England with the *Lyon*, 1631 (Dudley Letter). He came again in 1635, settling at Scituate, but was soon out of sympathy

	sympathy with the intolerant religious practices of the Winthrop government. Went to England to get relief but failed. He died 1655/6 at Barbados.
Vassall, Anne	Wife of William. Daughter of George King of Cold Norton, Essex (G.R., LXXV, 236).
Vassall, Judith	Child of William.
Vassall, Francis	Child of William.
Vassall, John	Child of William.
Vassall, Anne	Child of William.
WADE, (THOMAS)	Probably the person of this name of North-ampton who was an Adventurer of the Massachusetts Bay Company and came over to visit the country, returning with the Fleet. His stock in the Company was claimed by members of his family (Savage, IV, 377).
WALKER, ROBERT *Boston*	From Manchester, England. Linen weaver. Born 1601. Deposed 1679, aged 78 years. Member church, No. 131 (Sewall). Freeman 19 May 1634 (M.C.R., I, 369). Died 29 May 1687.
Walker, Sarah	Wife of Robert.
WALL, ——	In Winthrop's list. Returned with family (W).
Wall, ——	Wife of preceding.
——, ——	Servant of Mr. Wall.
WARD, THOMAS *Dedham*	Probably from Bedingham, co. Norfolk. Juror 28 Sept. 1630 (M.C.R., I, 78).
WARREN, JOHN *Watertown*	From Nayland, Suffolk (Stone Gen., 43). Freeman 18 May, 1631 (M.C.R., I, 366). Born 1585; died 13 (10) 1667 (W).
Warren, Margaret	Wife of John. Died 6 Nov. 1662.
WATERBURY, WILLIAM *Boston*	From Sudbury, co. Suffolk. Member First Church, No. 35.
Waterbury, Alice	Wife of William. Member First Church, No. 36.

WATERS, JOHN

WATERS, JOHN *Charlestown*	From Nayland, Suffolk. Member First Church, No. 23. Died soon. Winthrop called him 'my old servant' (Winthrop MSS., W. 7a. 47).
Waters, Frances	Wife of John. Member First Church, No. 24. Died soon.
Waters, Mary	Daughter of John. Died soon (L. & L.W., II, 54).
Waters, ——	Child of John (*ibid.*).
Waters, ——	Child of John (*ibid.*).
WEAVER, ——	Sent back to England 1631 (M.C.R., I, 82).
WEBB, RICHARD *Cambridge*	From Nayland, Suffolk. Freeman November 1632 (M.C.R., I, 367). Removed to Hartford.
Webb, Elizabeth	Wife of Richard. Member church, No. 120.
WEED, JONAS *Watertown*	Origin undetermined. Freeman 18 May 1631 (M.C.R., I, 366). Removed to Wethersfield, 1636, Stamford, 1642, and Southampton, L.I., 1657, where he died.
WEILLUST, JOIST *Boston*	Probably from Holland. Surveyor of Ordnance and cannonier. In June 1632 he was allowed five pounds towards the cost of transportation 'into his owne country' (M.C.R., I, 97).
WELDON, ROBERT *Charlestown*	Captain in the military service. Died 16 Feb. 1630/1 and was given a military funeral (Dudley Letter).
Weldon, Elizabeth	Wife of Capt. Robert. Member of First Church, No. 91. Marked 'gone to Watertown.'
WESTON, FRANCIS *Salem*	Origin undetermined. Freeman 5 Nov. 1633 (M.C.R., I, 368). Became an adherent to Mrs. Anne Hutchinson and was banished. Removed to Rhode Island. Richard Harcourt of Warwick, R.I., called Francis Weston and his wife 'my uncle and Aunt' (Documentary Hist., R.I.).
	Weston, Margaret

Weston, Margaret	Wife of Francis.
Weston, Lucy	Daughter of Francis. Married John Pease of Salem and Edgartown, Mass. (Banks, Hist. Martha's Vineyard, I, 89–103; II, 91–103).
WILBORE, SAMUEL *Boston*	Perhaps from London. Freeman 3 March 1633/4 (M.C.R., I, 368). He became an adherent of Mrs. Anne Hutchinson, was disarmed and removed to Rhode Island.
Wilbore, Anne	Wife of Samuel.
WILKINSON, PRUDENCE *Charlestown*	A widow. Origin unknown, but probably came with some relative not identified (Charlestown Town Rec.). Her will dated 9 Feb. 1655/6.
Wilkinson, Sarah	Daughter of Widow Prudence. Married William Bucknam.
Wilkinson, John	Son of Widow Prudence. Married Joan Skelton (E. & W.).
Wilkinson, Elizabeth	Daughter of Widow Prudence. Married George Felt (Felt Gen.).
WILLIAMS, THOMAS *Charlestown*	Origin undetermined. Juror 18 Sept. 1630 (M.C.R., I, 78). Ferryman. Freeman 18 May 1631 (M.C.R., I, 366). No further definite record.
WILLIAMS, THOMAS alias HARRIS	May be identical with preceding, but nothing further is positively known of him except that he applied for freeman 19 Oct. 1630 (M.C.R., I, 80). See HARRIS.
Williams, Robert	Perhaps son of Thomas; granted ferry license, 1641, (M.C.R., I, 341).
WILSBY, ——	In Winthrop's list, but no further record.
WILSON, JOHN *Boston*	Clergyman (M.C.R., I, 73). Son of Rev. William Wilson, Canon of St. George's Chapel, Windsor, but came from Sudbury, co. Suffolk. Pastor of the First Church, Boston.

WILTON, DAVID

WILTON, DAVID	Mentioned 1632. Removed to Windsor, Conn. where he died 5 Feb. 1677/8. Freeman 11 June 1633 (M.C.R., I, 368).
WING, ELIZABETH	Member church, No. 143.
WINTHROP, JOHN *Boston*	The Governor. From Groton, co. Suffolk.
Winthrop, Henry	Son of Gov. Winthrop. Drowned at Salem, 2 July 1630.
Winthrop, Stephen	Son of Gov. Winthrop (G.R., LXXV, 236).
Winthrop, Samuel	Son of Gov. Winthrop (G.R., LXXV, 236).
——, ——	
——, ——	
——, ——	
——, ——	
——, ——	(Eight servants of Gov. Winthrop, names unknown) (Winthrop Journal, 1853, I, 455).
——, ——	
——, ——	
WOODS, WILLIAM *Boston*	Not identified and origin unknown. Freeman 18 May 1631 (M.C.R., I, 366). In Winthrop's list.
WOOLRICH, JOHN *Charlestown*	Probably from London. Applied freeman 19 Oct. 1630 (M.C.R., I, 80). Freeman 4 March 1633/4 (M.C.R., I, 368).
Woolrich, Sarah	Wife of John. Member of First Church, No. 58. She married (2) William Ayre.
WORMEWOOD, ——	Sent back to England 1 March 1630/1 (M.C.R., I, 82).
WRIGHT, RICHARD *Boston*	Probably from Ratcliffe, Stepney, London. Member First Church, No. 89. Servant of John Humfrey (L. & L.W.). Freeman 14 May 1634 (M.C.R., I, 369).
Wright, Margaret	Wife of Richard. Married 8 Jan. 1625/6 at Stepney. Member of First Church, No. 99.
Wright, Eleanor	Daughter of Richard. Testified 29 Dec. 1701 aged 80 years, that she came over with her

her father, Richard Wright, in the first ship, to Boston, when she was 9 or 10 years old. She married Richard Clarke.

WRIGHT, ROBERT   Citizen and merchant tailor from London. Sent back under arrest in ship *Lyon* April 1631 for 'treason' and 'clipping coins' (Suffolk Court Files, XLV, 12).

APPENDIX B

PASSENGERS OF THE *MARY AND JOHN* IN 1630

CONTEMPORANEOUSLY with the sailing of the Winthrop Fleet a party of emigrants embarked at Plymouth, Devon, in the ship *Mary and John*, on March 20, bound for the same destination in Massachusetts Bay within the bounds of the territory of the Company headed by Winthrop. While not having any defined connection with the Winthrop Fleet, yet their destination presupposes a coöperative agreement and a common purpose.[1] In his last letter to his wife, before leaving Southampton, Winthrop notes the departure of this vessel and her passengers, indicating his knowledge of their destination in the limits of the Massachusetts Bay Patent and by inference an approval of them as fellow emigrants under his jurisdiction. The *Mary and John* was owned by Roger Ludlow, one of the Assistants of the Massachusetts Bay Company, who sailed in her, as did Edward Rossiter, another Assistant, as leaders of this Company, and thus further confirmation is given to it as an integral, though separated, part of the Great Emigration. It seems, therefore, desirable to relate briefly the story of this group which on arrival settled on Dorchester Neck and soon became politically merged in the fortunes of the various groups which reached our shores in that year.

The Reverend John White, Vicar of Dorchester, England, who has been generally and rightfully acclaimed as the sponsor of the earliest Massachusetts settlement (Plymouth excepted), was the inspiration of a movement which culminated in the gathering of nearly one hundred and fifty persons in the counties of Dorset, Somerset, and Devon and their agreement to emigrate in a body to Massachusetts whither he had sent other groups in the previous six years. White was a Conforming Puritan who believed that the religious unrest of the period could be better composed by a liberal attitude of all factions within the Established Church. He was strongly against separation and the creation of independent religious bodies and severely condemned the subsequent action of Winthrop and Cotton who were promoting religious intolerance in Massachusetts.

His influence in the West Country was widespread and in this, his latest effort to encourage colonization in New England, he not only secured recruits in his own city and county but in the adjoining counties of Devon and

[1] The Reverend Francis Higginson in a letter sent back to England in July, 1629, reported that information had been sent to Endicott notifying him that sixty families of 'Dorcettershire' intended to sail next spring with their ministers for the Colony and he was requested 'to appoint them places of habitation.'

and the remote parts of Somerset. In describing this Company he said that scarce a half-dozen of them were personally known to each other prior to their assembling at the place of embarkation in Plymouth. (Planter's Plea, 37.) There they first came to a personal acquaintance with those who were to be their companions on the voyage and neighbors in the New World during the rest of their days. It may be assumed that these people, from many parishes scattered over three counties, were moved by the same urge to emigrate which animated those of the Winthrop Fleet, but it is safe to say that the tales of 'religious persecution' of these people was not a factor in their pilgrimage. The West Country was free from it.

With them went two clergymen of the Established Church, one the Reverend John Maverick, at that time Vicar of Beaworthy, Devon, son of a clergyman and then in his fifty-eighth year. Already his son, Samuel, had been a resident of Massachusetts for seven years and was living in what is now Chelsea. This probably explains his emigration with the *Mary and John* Company, bringing with him his large family to be near his eldest son. There is nothing in any existing record to indicate that Maverick was unfaithful to his oath at ordination to conduct himself conformably and follow the prescribed ritual of the Church service. Like White he was a conformist, though liberal in his attitude on controverted subjects. The other clergyman, the Reverend John Warham, was fourteen years the junior of Maverick, and of a different quality. He was a native, probably, of Crewkerne, Somerset, born about 1592, had taken holy orders, and came under the ecclesiastical jurisdiction of Laud, then Bishop of Bath and Wells. It is not necessary to state that this famous church official, later to be Archbishop of Canterbury, was a strict disciplinarian in matters of conformity to canon law, and Warham soon fell under his displeasure for some contumacy and was suspended. He removed to Exeter, where under the more liberal Bishop Hall he was given the parish of Saint Sidwell, a living which he held until his emigration. He was an aggressive theologian.

The intending emigrants having assembled at Plymouth were met by White and by courtesy of the Reverend Matthias Nicolls, Master of the New Hospital, an old friend of the 'Patriarch of Dorchester,' they gathered in the chapel where services were conducted and a farewell sermon was preached by him as sponsor of the movement.[1] This was on Saturday, March 20,

---

[1] The claim that these emigrants formed a separatist church at Plymouth prior to sailing is entirely contrary to the facts and is based on a misinterpretation of the language used by one of the party. Before leaving they chose the two clergymen as 'officers' of the Company, not of a church, and on arrival they served as town officials, granting lands and transacting town business, like Selectmen, a duty never performed by ministers of regular churches. The Dorchester Church was not 'gathered' as a Separatist body until after arrival in New England, being the third Sep-
aratist

March 20, and at its conclusion they embarked to set sail for the distant shores of an unknown country. The *Mary and John* made a good passage and arrived at Nantasket May 30 without casualty. These one hundred and forty passengers are generally known as the Dorchester Company, from the place chosen for their settlement, and as they remained a distinct body of colonists, and there are contemporary records to identify most of them, it has been possible to compile a tentative list of those who came on this pioneer ship. Five years later a great majority of them removed to Windsor, Connecticut, under the leadership of Warham.

The following list shows the names of heads of families and the number in each family sailing in this ship. It gives the county of origin and the place of settlement after arrival, with other notes of identification. The list shows that fifteen came from Somerset, fifteen from Dorset, six from Devon and three are of undetermined origin. The total number thus listed makes one hundred and thirty-four out of the one hundred and forty who came over. The figures after each name indicates the number of persons in the emigrant's family.

Key to Abbreviations

Stiles	History of Windsor, Conn.
Blake	History of Dorchester, Mass.
Pope	Pioneers of Massachusetts
M.C.R.	Massachusetts Colonial Records
Clapp	Memoirs of Roger Clapp

BASKOM, THOMAS (1)   Dorset. Removed to Windsor (Stiles).

COOKE, AARON (1)   Dorset. A minor, stepson of Thomas Ford (see below). Removed to Windsor (Stiles).

CLAPP, ROGER (1)   Devon. Settled at Dorchester. Freeman 14 May 1634 (M.C.R., I, 368); Died 2 Feb. 1690/1 (Clapp).

DENSLOW, NICHOLAS (3)   Dorset. Removed to Windsor (Stiles).

DYER, GEORGE (4)   Somerset. Settled Dorchester; constable 1630; Freeman 18 May 1631 (M.C.R., I, 366). Died 1672 (Blake).

DRAKE, JOHN (6)

aratist church in order after Salem and Boston. Edward Johnson, who lived at the time and wrote from personal knowledge, distinctly states this in his well-known historical work. (*Wonder-Working Providence of Sion's Savior in New England*, C, xii.)

DRAKE, JOHN (6) — Devon. Removed to Windsor (Stiles).

DUNCAN, NATHANIEL (4) — Devon. Settled Dorchester. Freeman 6 May 1635 (M.C.R., I, 370); died 1668 (Pope).

FORD, THOMAS (6) — Dorset. Applied freeman 19 Oct. 1630 (M.C.R., I, 81); freeman 18 May 1631 (*ibid.*, I, 366). Removed to Windsor (Stiles).

GAYLORD, WILLIAM (4) — Somerset. Juror 1630. Freeman 18 May 1631 (M.C.R., I, 366). Deacon of church. Removed to Windsor (Blake, Stiles).

GALLOP, HUMPHREY (2) — Dorset. Settled Dorchester (Pope).

GALLOP, JOHN (4) — Dorset. Settled Boston. Freeman 1 April 1634 (M.C.R., I, 368).

GIBBS, GILES (7) — Dorset. Freeman 4 March 1632/3 (M.C.R. I, 367). Removed to Windsor where he died 1641 (Stiles).

GILLETT, JONATHAN (1) — Somerset. Freeman 6 May 1635 (M.C.R., I, 370). Removed to Windsor (Stiles).

GREENWAY, JOHN (7) — Origin undetermined. Applied freeman 19 Oct. 1630 (M.C.R., I, 80); freeman 18 May 1631 (*ibid.*, I, 366). Settled Dorchester and died there about 1652 (Gen. Reg., IX, 348; XXXII, 55).

HANNUM, WILLIAM (1) — Dorset. Removed to Windsor where he died 1677 (Stiles).

HILL, WILLIAM (2) — Dorset. Freeman 5 Nov. 1633 (Pope).

HOLMAN, JOHN (1) — Dorset. Settled Dorchester. No record as freeman. Died 1652 (Gen. Reg.).

HOSKINS, JOHN (4) — Origin undetermined. Freeman 18 May 1631 (M.C.R., I, 366). Removed to Windsor (Pope).

HULL, GEORGE (4)

HULL, GEORGE (4)	Somerset. Freeman 4 March 1632/3 (M.C.R., I, 367). Removed to Windsor (Blake).
LOVELL, WILLIAM (2)	Somerset. Captain; settled Dorchester (Pope).
LUDLOW, ROGER (6)	Wiltshire. Assistant of the Mass. Bay Company; Deputy Governor of Massachusetts. Removed to Windsor and later to Virginia (Pope).
MAVERICK, REVEREND JOHN (7)	Devon. Applied freeman 19 Oct. 1630 (M.C.R., I, 180); freeman 18 May 1631 (*ibid.*, I, 366). Settled Dorchester. Died 3 Feb. 1635/6 (Pope).
MOORE, JOHN (1)	Origin unknown. Settled Dorchester. Freeman 18 May 1631 (M.C.R., I, 366). Removed to Windsor (Stiles).
PHELPS, GEORGE (1)	Dorset. Freeman 6 May 1635 (M.C.R., I, 371). Removed to Windsor (Stiles).
PHELPS, WILLIAM (6)	Dorset. Juror 1630. Freeman 18 May 1631 (M.C.R., I, 366). Removed to Windsor (Stiles).
PINNEY, HUMPHREY (2)	Somerset. Freeman 14 May 1634 (M.C.R., I, 369). Removed to Windsor (Stiles).
POMEROY, ELTWEED (3)	Somerset. Freeman 4 March 1632/3 (M.C.R., I, 367). Removed to Windsor (Pomeroy Gen.).
RICHARDS, THOMAS (6)	Probably Somerset. Settled Dorchester. Freeman 13 May 1640 (M.C.R., I, 377). Removed to Weymouth where he died 1650 (Blake).
ROCKWELL, WILLIAM (4)	Somerset. Freeman 18 May 1631 (M.C.R., I, 366). Deacon of church. Removed to Windsor (Rockwell Gen.).
ROSSITER, BRIAN (1)	Somerset. Freeman 18 May 1631 (M.C.R., I, 366). Removed to Windsor (Clapp).
	ROSSITER, EDWARD (4)

ROSSITER, EDWARD (4)	Somerset. Assistant of Massachusetts Bay Company. Died 1630 (Pope).
SOUTHCOTE, RICHARD (1)	Devon. Captain; freeman 18 May 1631 (M.C.R., I, 366). Returned to England.
SYLVESTER, RICHARD (1)	Somerset. Applied freeman 1630 (M.C.R., I, 80). Settled Dorchester. Freeman 1 April 1634 (*ibid.*, I, 368). Removed to Weymouth. Died 1663 (Pope).
TERRY, STEPHEN (3)	Dorset. Nephew of Rev. John White. Freeman 18 May 1631 (M.C.R., I, 366). Removed to Windsor (Terry Gen.).
TILLEY, JOHN (2)	Somerset. Settled Dorchester. Freeman 4 May 1634/5 (M.C.R., I, 370). Died soon (Blake).
UPSALL, NICHOLAS (1)	Dorset. Settled Dorchester. Juror 1630. Freeman 18 May 1631 (M.C.R., I, 366). Died Aug. 1666, aged about 73 (Pope).
WARHAM, REVEREND JOHN (4)	Devon. Applied freeman 19 Oct. 1630 (M.C.R., I, 80); freeman 18 May 1631 (*ibid.*, I, 366). Removed to Windsor where he died 1 April 1670 (Stiles, Blake).
WAY, HENRY (6)	Dorset. Settled Dorchester. No record as to freeman. Died 1667 (Blake).
WILLIAMS, ROGER (2)	Somerset. This person is not to be confounded with the famous clergyman of same name. Freeman 18 May 1631 (M.C.R., I, 366). Removed to Windsor (Pope).
WOLCOTT, HENRY (8)	Somerset. Applied freeman 19 Oct. 1630 (M.C.R., I, 79); freeman 1 April 1634 (*ibid.*, I, 368). Removed to Windsor (Stiles).

Note: From the above tabulation it appears that of the 40 heads of families who came in this ship 13 remained permanently in Dorchester, 23 removed to Windsor, Connecticut with Warham, in the migration of 1635-36, and 4 settled elsewhere in Massachusetts.

APPENDIX C

THE SHIP *LYON*, 1630

This ship was famous in the history of the early emigration to Massachusetts, and her Master was equally noted for his skillful seamanship and his sympathy with the policy of the Puritan leaders. In 1630, 1631, and 1632 she made four voyages hither in quick succession under his command with the regularity and safety of a ferry, and on one of them saved the new settlement from starvation and death by her timely arrival with provisions and anti-scorbutics. The official connection of the *Lyon* with the Winthrop Fleet is of the same character as related of the *Mary and John*, as both were doubtless approved by the Governor and Assistants. In his letter of March 28, 1630 to his wife, written from the *Arbella*, off the Isle of Wight, after noting the sailing of the *Mary and John*, Winthrop wrote: 'and the ship which goes from Bristowe (Bristol) carrieth about eighty persons.' (L.L.W., I, 388). This was the *Lyon* and she probably sailed from that port to accommodate passengers living in the West Counties — Lancashire, Cheshire, Warwick, Gloucestershire, and Somerset. That they were authorized to settle in the limits of the Bay Patent seems assured, as there is no evidence to the contrary following their arrival. The date of her departure is not known (probably in March) but her arrival at Salem is reported 'in the latter part of May' (Bradford, II, 67), some time before the *Arbella* reached that port. The identity of this ship is not established as there were several of her name in existence at that period. In view of her valuable services to the Colony it is to be hoped that the necessary search may be made to fix her home port, previous history, tonnage, and ownership.

Of Captain William Peirse, her Master, more particulars are known. He had sailed to Plymouth in 1623 as Master of the *Anne* of London, bringing the last lot of passengers to the Pilgrim settlement. He was then a resident of Ratcliffe, parish of Stepney, London, and at that date was about thirty-one years old. He made a voyage to Salem in 1629 as Master of the *Mayflower* (not the Pilgrim ship) and thereafter he was in constant traffic in passengers and merchandise across the Atlantic. He took up his residence in Boston in 1632 and was admitted freeman 14 May 1634 (M.C.R., I, 369). His wife, Bridget, joined the church 2 Feb. 1632/3; perhaps a second wife, as a William Peirce, mariner of Whitechapel, was licensed in 1615 to marry Margaret Gibbs. Whitechapel and Stepney are adjoining parishes. He became a Town and Colony official and was engaged in coastwise shipping thereafter. He compiled an Almanac for New England

England which was the second issue in 1639 from the Daye press at Cambridge. In 1641 he was killed by the Spaniards while on a voyage to the island of New Providence, Bahamas Group, whither he was taking passengers for settlement.

The names and identities of the eighty passengers who sailed in the *Lyon* from Bristol to Salem have not been investigated, as they were soon amalgamated with the existing settlement there and it would require long and special study to segregate them from the 'Old Planters' and the more recent emigrants who came with Endicott.

APPENDIX D

CAPTAIN PETER MILBURNE OF THE *ARBELLA*

THE Master of the Admiral of the Winthrop Fleet who successfully led this great flotilla to its destination deserves particular mention as an actor in the drama of early emigration to New England, as Christopher Jones, the Master of the *Mayflower* of 1620, has been acclaimed for bringing the Pilgrims in safety to Plymouth. Peter Milburne was a resident of London, in the parish of St. Katherine by the Tower, but beyond this, little information about him or his family has come to light. He was probably of London origin, as the family name is found there before 1600, and his residence on the water-front seems to confirm this suggestion. Stepney, the sailors' parish, was the next neighboring one on the east, and there he married, on August 3, 1615, the widow Jane Coulter of Wapping, a hamlet of Stepney. Presumably he was master of the *Eagle* when she was bought for the voyage overseas, and the name changed to *Arbella*. That he was not only a skillful, but a popular sea-captain is evident from the testimony of Governor Winthrop. In a letter to his son after arrival here he sent this message:

> 'We had a comfortable passage and I found that love and respect from Capt. Milburne our master, as I may not forget. I pray, (if he be returned before you come hither,) take occasion to see him and remember my kind salutations to him and his wife.' ('Life and Letters of John Winthrop,' II, 40).

It is not known whether he or his vessel ever returned to these waters, nor anything of his later career, but it may be hoped that some future chronicler will be able to add to this brief record the full story of the life of the senior captain of this Fleet, so pleasantly remembered by the senior official of the Massachusetts Bay Company.

APPENDIX E

MRS. ANNE (——) POLLARD

THIS passenger, according to her own story, came with the Winthrop Fleet of 1630 in one of the first ships that arrived at Charlestown. She was then about nine or ten years of age and described herself as 'a romping girl' of the type who would be the heroine of the special incident which will be her title to enduring local fame. She is credited with being the first female, of all the passengers, to set foot on the peninsula of Shawmut, now the city of Boston, and for that reason deserves special notice in this story of the Great Emigration. Taking one of the ship's boats, with a party of young people, she went over to Shawmut in search of fresh water, as the springs at Charlestown gave a brackish, unpalatable, and inadequate water supply. As the boat touched the shore, she was the first to leap out, and her claim to priority of landing in Boston has been of record for more than a century.

She became the wife of William Pollard, innholder of Boston, by whom she had a large family, and at her death, December 6, 1725, she had nearly reached the great age of one hundred and five years. Franklin's 'New England Courant' in a short obituary notice of this centenarian stated that she was born in Saffron Walden, Essex, but with this clue it has not been possible, up to the time of the issue of this volume, to identify her among the many children baptized 'Anne' in the years calculated from her age at death. None of the various parents of all these Annes can be recognized as coming to Boston with her, either by name or connected with her by will here or in England, after extensive investigation by one of the leading genealogists of London. The matter is still being followed up. Her portrait, painted when she became a centenarian, is in the collections of the Massachusetts Historical Society and a reproduction may be seen in Bolton's 'Portraits of the Founders.'

INDEXES

INDEX OF NAMES

INDEX OF PLACES

INDEX OF SUBJECTS

CPSIA information can be obtained at www.ICGtesting.com
Printed in the USA
BVOW08s0752150813

328594BV00008B/107/P